PRIVATIZING
FEDERAL SPENDING

PRIVATIZING FEDERAL SPENDING

A Strategy to Eliminate the Deficit

Stuart M. Butler

UNIVERSE BOOKS
New York

Acknowledgments

I am grateful for the assistance of many people for their contributions to this book. Particular thanks should go to my research assistant, Jeffrey Smith, for his painstaking work. In addition, Karen Albers, Graydon Frick, and Stephen Moore played critical roles in preparing the final manuscript.

My thanks go also to Burton Pines and the staff of The Heritage Foundation, who made it possible for me to combine writing this book with my other duties at the Foundation.

Published in the United States of America in 1985
by Universe Books
381 Park Avenue South, New York, N.Y. 10016

85 86 87 88 89 / 10 9 8 7 6 5 4 3 2 1

Printed in the United States of America

Library of Congress Cataloging in Publication Data

Butler, Stuart M.
   Privatizing federal spending.

   Includes index.
   1. United States—Appropriations and expenditures.
2. Government spending policy—United States.
3. Budget deficits—United States. I. Title.
HJ2052.B87   1985   339.5'23'0973   84-8805
ISBN 0-87663-454-4

Contents

Introduction

There is no shortage of support in America for the idea of cutting the size of the federal government. Nor is there any lack of studies showing that waste and inefficiency pervade government programs, implying that the public sector could be reduced while maintaining, or even improving, the level of goods and services. But there is one missing ingredient in the campaign for a smaller and more efficient government sector—a political strategy that works.

The election of Ronald Reagan in 1980 seemed like the dawn of a new era to the advocates of limited government. To the liberal establishment, of course, it was more like the barbarians closing in upon Rome. The Washington of January, 1981 was full of confident talk of balanced budgets and a historic reversal of the growth of federal spending. And on the cocktail circuit, no topic of conversation was more in vogue than the contents of David Stockman's budget briefing books.

After four years of Ronald Reagan, however, deficits have reached once unimaginable levels and the tough talk about spending has all but disappeared. The rhetoric may still be the same, if subdued, but one can almost feel the shell shock affecting the administration and its closest supporters. In his first four years President Reagan rang up a cumulative deficit equal to nearly half the total red ink amassed by all his predecessors since World War II. Worse still, from the point of view of those wishing to turn back the tide of government, the Washington bureaucracy consumes even more of the nation's income than it did under Jimmy Carter.

It is clear that the Reagan administration, and its allies in Congress have all but conceded the battle to cut the federal budget. By election day 1984 David Stockman was no longer the ruthless program cutter of four years earlier, and congressional Republicans seemed to have given up the fight. Inch by inch the Reaganites were pushed toward the one method of reducing the deficit that they claimed they would never consider—raising taxes.

The reaction of conservatives to this development ranges from grim acceptance to bitter denunciations. To some, Reagan's budget failure shows a lack of resolve, an unwillingness to mobilize the people and to play hardball with Congress. To some, it demonstrates too great a dependency by the president on officials and advisers who have never totally accepted his view of limited government. Others believe that they simply supported the wrong man for the job and that a truly determined president in the White House, with enough sympathizers elected to Congress, could cut government down to size. Still others such as Nobel Laureate Milton Friedman feel that even this would not be enough unless Congress were also shackled with a constitutional amendment to balance the budget and constrain spending.

The underlying cause of the Reagan administration's failure to control the federal budget under existing constitutional arrangements, however, can hardly be blamed on a lack of backbone or commitment to ideology. Nor is it rooted in any inability or unwillingness to identify programs that could be reduced or eliminated. It has been due, instead, to the failure of officials to get a grip on the basic political dynamics of budget growth. Just as the administration saw the need to devise a tax policy to stimulate the supply side of the private economy, so it took what one might call a supply-side view of the budget process. This view held that budget control consisted of reducing the supply of funds available to programs and individuals by requesting less money from Congress and then winning the votes necessary to legislate those cuts. Some advocates of this position also argued that if beneficial and popular tax reductions could first be enacted and tax revenues decreased, the prospect of looming deficits (perhaps amounting to as much as $100 billion a year!) surely would force Congress to slash spending in line with White House demands.

Needless to say, this did not happen. The reason is that the supply-side approach to budget cutting overlooks two facts: It is the *demand* for government services that powers the growth of government, and there is a systematic political imbalance between those who desire more spending and those who desire less—an imbalance consistently favoring the pro-spending lobby. As we shall see in Chapter 1, a powerful coalition of beneficiaries, service suppliers, political activists, and bureaucrats tends to develop around each federal spending program. It is in the interest of those coalitions to press for an expansion of the federal role. Each program expansion that is won from Congress widens the coalition's power, enabling it to seek ever more funding for its programs. When an administration tries to cut back funding for activities, the coalition swings into action to throw a block on the move. It is a tight group with a lot to lose if the cuts go through—so it fights long and it fights hard.

The cost of such programs, however, is spread thinly over all taxpayers. Several million dollars to create a new federal service, or to expand an existing one, translates into a few cents for the average taxpayer. That taxpayer may complain about taxes in general, but the impact of any one particular federal program is rarely sufficient to spur the taxpayer into angry opposition. And even if it does, the individual is unlikely to be able to draw together a group of fellow taxpayers sufficiently strong and focused to alter the political balance in their favor. The politician in Washington may have much to lose by opposing a well-organized lobby of program beneficiaries, but that same politician will rarely face the same potential threat from the individual taxpayer.

The same imbalance holds true when there is talk of reducing federal outlays. Everyone professes to be in favor of greater efficiency. But when it comes to the details, the political dynamics always tend to favor spending over efficiency. The coalition benefiting from a program has a strong financial incentive to mount a well-organized campaign carefully directed at the most vulnerable legislators. But any savings likely to accrue from canceling a program may take years to materialize, and they will be spread thinly over a hundred million taxpayers. In fact, in an era of generally rising taxes, the taxpayer is unlikely to detect any benefit whatsoever if a federal expenditure is reduced. With such an imbalance between the impact on gainers and the effect on losers, it is hard to amass decisive political support for cutting out even the most outrageous waste, let alone paring back a program that is merely extravagant.

The Reagan administration has not been unaware of these lopsided political dynamics. In fact, administration officials and conservative politicians routinely denounce the unfairness of it all. Yet budget tacticians have been unable to devise a strategy to reverse the growth of government. They have certainly scored some successes, most notably by using the Great Communicator in the White House to rally the country's taxpayers. But such occasional victories pale into insignificance beside the countless defeats suffered in the budget war of attrition.

Unless the administration is able to cut the federal budget, there seems little doubt that deficits will grow and that political momentum to raise taxes will prove unstoppable. If that happens, the very foundation of Reagan's plan to halt the growth of government will have been destroyed. But the administration will never be able to reverse the growth of spending until it learns from its opponents and switches from a supply-side budget strategy to a demand-side approach. It must, in other words, abandon the idea of trying to hold down spending by attempting to apply and sustain spending ceilings. That is a little like trying to stop a pot from boiling over by pressing down on the lid. You can stop a pot from boiling over only by cutting off the supply of heat, and you can stop government spending only by turning down the demand for its goods and services.

A strategy for cutting the demand for spending is laid out in the following pages. It must consist of several elements if it is to be successful, but it centers on one central theme—privatization. The privatization strategy tackles the spending coalitions head on, by diverting the demand for government goods and services out of the public sector and into the nongovernment sector. But in contrast to the unsuccessful approach—trying to do this simply by eliminating existing federal services—privatization seeks to accomplish the task by first establishing private-sector alternatives that are more attractive to the current supporters of government programs. By providing incentives to the suppliers and beneficiaries of these alternative services, privatization aims to create a mirror image of the political coalitions that lead to an ever larger federal role. These private-sector coalitions, like those currently pushing for new or bigger government programs, would also have powerful incentives to press for an expansion of programs that benefit their constituents—but in this case the programs would be outside the federal orbit.

By redirecting key segments of the demand for federal spending in this way, and thus weakening the coalitions for federal programs, the political balance between the taxpayers and the program beneficiaries is made more favorable to budget cutting. With this reduction in demand-side pressure, a rational debate could take place on ways to economize in the supply of government services. Once the demand pressure for government spending is reduced, moreover, the political opposition to sensible budget reductions is also reduced. In other words, privatization would prepare the political ground for traditional budget-cutting approaches to succeed.

It is very difficult for politicians in a democracy to retain office by promising their constituents fewer goods and services. The architects of the administration's budget-cutting strategy have slowly come to realize this. The reaction to this political fact of life was intense frustration, combined with a desperate determination to dig in and hold the line on spending. But a purely defensive strategy is bound to fail in the long run. The privatization technique offers an opportunity to outflank the supporters of bigger government by turning the current political dynamics upside down. If Ronald Reagan's administration is to represent a fundamental change in the role of government and not just an interesting footnote in the history books, privatization is a technique that must be utilized quickly and decisively.

WHY REAGAN HAS NOT CUT THE BUDGET

The Failure of the Supply-Side Approach

Ronald Reagan entered the White House in 1981 with a fierce determination to bring the burgeoning federal government under tight control. The goal was a balanced budget and a decline in the proportion of the nation's resources preempted by the federal government. The Reagan administration also sought to implement a version of the Kemp-Roth across-the-board federal tax-cut proposal, so that the steady inflation-driven bracket creep of the 1970s would be halted and incentives to save and take risks would be restored.

The Reagan administration scored a remarkable congressional victory in 1981 with the passage of the Economic Recovery Tax Act (ERTA), which provided for a 25% cut in personal tax rates over three years and indexed those rates for inflation beginning in 1985. ERTA also improved depreciation schedules and other business allowances. While ERTA was by no means the massive tax cut some of its supporters and opponents have claimed, it did begin to edge total federal taxation down toward the proportion of GNP that prevailed in the early 1970s.

If the total tax burden was to be cut under the Reagan administration and the federal budget brought into balance, then clearly the level of federal spending had to be brought down at least as quickly as taxes. Consequently, the Reagan forces moved quickly after the inauguration to push through Congress a package of budget reductions devised by David Stockman's Office of Management and Budget. The 1981 budget cuts were to be the first install-ment of a series of packages designed to bring down federal spending well below 20% of GNP.

It was this spending side of the Reagan equation that went seri-ously awry. After some success in 1981, the White House seemed completely to lose control of the budget. To say that the adminis-tration missed its target would be a colossal understatement. As Table 1 shows, the Reagan administration was not merely unable to reduce federal spending as a percentage of GNP; the propor-tion has actually *risen* rapidly, reaching a historic high in 1983 unsurpassed even during wartime. Ronald Reagan is now on record as the big spender to end all big spenders—an irony indeed for such a conservative politician.

Contrary to the impression created by some critics of the Reagan administration, this expansion has not been due to dramatic increases in defense spending that overshadowed deep cuts in social programs. Defense expenditures certainly have increased under Reagan. Between fiscal year (FY) 1981 and FY 1983 the increase was 1% of GNP (from 5.5% to 6.5%). But transfer payments to individuals also rose by 1% of GNP over the same period. Moreover, as pointed out in a major 1984 study by the Woodrow Wilson School at Princeton University, in many instances the states replaced the money that was cut from specific federal domestic programs.[1]

Table 1

Growth of Federal Spending under the Reagan Administration (as a percentage of GNP)

Fiscal Year*	1980 Carter Projections	1981 Reagan Projections	Actual Spending
1981	22.3	22.6	22.8
1982	22.1	22.3	23.8
1983	22.0	22.0	24.7
1984	—	21.4	23.5

*The fiscal year begins in October of the preceding calendar year.

Source: Carter estimates: *Budget of the United States Government* (Fiscal Year 1981); Reagan estimates: *Budget of the United States Government* (Fiscal Year 1982); Actuals: *Budget of the United States Government* (Fis-cal Year 1985), Office of Management and Budget.

It is not easy to determine from the raw numbers of Table 1, however, exactly what has happened to spending on specific segments of the American population. But Milton Friedman has attempted to identify the impact on certain groups, and his findings are somewhat surprising. Friedman examined welfare programs that benefit the poor, such as Aid to Families with Dependent Children, Supplemental Security Income, food stamps, and housing subsidies. He discovered that, on the whole, federal welfare spending has been held remarkably constant under Ronald Reagan as a fraction of GNP. However, "Welfare for the middle class and upper income class," as Friedman puts it—programs such as Medicare, federal retirement, and spending on higher education—has gone up sharply. The only substantial decreases in spending, he says, were in programs largely administered by the states and localities, including transportation grants, certain programs in education, and development monies.[2] But the impact of these programs on particular classes is even harder to determine than are the effects of programs administered directly from Washington.

Looking at the overall picture, Friedman concludes that the Reaganites "have seen no progress towards [the president's] objectives of cutting government spending and balancing the budget. Even after the fullest possible allowance for the effect of the recession on government spending and the deficit, both spending and the deficit have continued to rise as a fraction of [national] income."[3]

The Reagan administration and its friends in the Congress evidently agree with analyses such as Friedman's. They gradually abandoned all hope of bringing federal spending down to the proportion of GNP typical in the 1970s (which would require total outlays to shrink by nearly one-fifth), let alone achieving their original objective of a dramatic rollback of the federal government. By 1984, budget director David Stockman had lost his enthusiasm for draconian cuts, believing instead that a new plateau had been reached in spending levels. He began to describe as "dreamers" those who continued to press for a determined attack on entitlements during a second Reagan term. In a 1984 *Fortune* interview, for instance, Stockman declared that "Our biggest failure was that we didn't create a bigger and better package of spending cuts in the beginning. We should have gone after the big boulders—the social insurance programs. The rest of the budget is thousands of little pebbles. But now the big items are impervious—they are social commitments."[4]

Stockman had felt that the only realistic budget strategy consisted of chipping away here and there at programs and perhaps trying to erode the purchasing power of Social Security and other entitlement programs by capping cost-of-living adjustments below the inflation rate. And by early 1984, Stockman had decided that Reagan's 1981 goal of reducing the size of the federal government below 20% of GNP was an impossible target. "I don't see how you can get government spending down to 19% of GNP," he concluded in the *Fortune* interview, "given the requirements for defense and what you can get out of the domestic side. The minimum size of government achievable appears to be 22% to 23% of GNP."[5]

Congressional support for program reductions also had evaporated by election year. Finance Committee Chairman Bob Dole summed up the consensus among Republicans when he asked at one set of hearings on the budget, "If you cannot touch Social Security and you cannot touch entitlements, and you cannot cut defense and you cannot control interest payments, what can you cut?" The first down payment on the budget deficit, enacted in the summer of 1984, reflected this view. Although it contained significant tax increases, the budget reductions were largely cosmetic.

The complete failure of the administration to achieve any significant budget cuts, combined with the dreadful prospect of annual deficits amounting to hundreds of billions of dollars, has steadily undermined support for the tax reductions enacted in 1981. Despite the lack of evidence that deficits per se force up interest rates or are particularly damaging to an economy, many White House officials, including Stockman and chief economist Martin Feldstein, joined the chorus demanding tax increases to bridge the deficit gap.[6] By election year, practically everybody in the administration—including Ronald Reagan—had turned a deaf ear to Milton Friedman's cautionary words, "You cannot reduce the deficit by raising taxes. Increasing taxes only results in more spending, leaving the deficit at the highest level accepted by the public. Political Rule No. 1 is: Government spends what government receives plus as much as it can get away with."[7]

By the time of the election campaign, the administration seemed reduced to merely token demands for budget cuts. No serious budget reductions have been obtained from Congress since 1981, and none seems likely in the near future. And instead of carefully crafted proposals to reform the budget process, the president appears unable to do anything more than denounce spendthrifts in Congress and grasp at the straw of a constitutional amendment to balance the budget and limit spending—for the moment an unlikely solution.

It would be hard to fault the 1981 Reagan administration, however, on its determination to follow through with its commitment to reduce the size of government. The failure of Ronald Reagan to achieve a decisive victory in the battle of the budget has had nothing to do with lack of will. But it has had much to do with obsolete weaponry. The initial and fundamental mistake of the administration was its assumption that the only way to control and cut the budget is to seek legislation to reduce the supply of dollars flowing out of Washington. This led the White House to view spending in aggregate terms and to regard the budget problem solely as one of managing and restraining expenditures.

The fatal flaw in this supply side view of the budget process is that it ignores the demand side of the political equation. It overlooks the subtle process by which government programs grow and the fact that they are sustained by powerful coalitions. When this process is examined, it becomes clear why no administration is likely to succeed in reducing the size of the federal budget by the conventional approach of seeking to win congressional backing for substantial spending cuts. A new strategy is needed.

Why Programs Grow

A New View of Federalism

The most significant upturn in federal spending occurred in the early 1930s. From the beginning of the century until the onset of the Great Depression, federal spending hovered around 3% of GNP. Total state government spending at that time was more than double the amount spent at the federal level. The United States was still as the Founding Fathers had envisioned it—a country in which state and local governments catered to most needs of the people, and in which the national government looked after matters truly national in scope, such as defense.

The proximate cause of the sudden and rapid growth of federal spending in the 1930s was certainly the government's determination to tackle the depression, but this is insufficient as a complete answer. It does not explain, for instance, why it was the federal government that expanded, and not state governments. Nor does it explain why federal spending continued to grow after World War II, when the severe economic problems of the depression years had disappeared.

An important element in the choice of the federal government as the vehicle for public spending was the triumph of the liberal view of federalism. As Alexis de Tocqueville had noted during his journeys to America, the triumph of the American federal system was that it managed to reconcile two contradictory sets of political principles. Federalists such as Madison and Hamilton maintained that a strong national government was essential for the prosperity of each citizen. The Anti-Federalists, in contrast, believed that freedom and the new Republic could survive only if the national government was weak and political power rested close to the citizens, in state and local institutions. They were scornful, moreover, of the strident individualism and pursuit of wealth favored by the Federalists. Only by shunning excessive individualism and sharing obligations, argued the Federalists, could the Republic remain civilized.

America resolved these contrasting views, Tocqueville observed, through its federal form of government. The national government promoted commercial interests. But it was balanced by a system of decentralized self-governing communities and voluntary associations that fostered public-spiritedness.

The twentieth-century liberal challenge to this view of American society maintained that the traditional balance between levels of government was outmoded. State and local government could no longer be counted on to discharge the obligations of a civilized community. According to the liberals, a sense of community should be created on a national scale, in such a way that the power of the national government, rather than individual goals, could be utilized to promote the public interest. Egalitarianism and national public virtue would characterize the actions of federal institutions—a goal the early Anti-Federalists believed to be unattainable.

The intellectual support for this radical version of federalism provided a strong impetus for the creation of national programs to meet the crisis of the 1930s, and it has been a consideration ever since. In keeping with the assumption that the national government is the embodiment of the compassionate community, social service programs have continued to grow rapidly. Even when these programs have utilized state and local governments to administer federal funds, tight guidelines have generally been applied in an effort to ensure that assistance reaches the truly needy—a reflection of the liberal contention that state and local governments pursue narrow interests and cannot be trusted to further the public interest.

The liberal view of federalism has provided the intellectual backdrop and the political rhetoric for the dramatic expansion of the federal government. But it is not responsible for the underlying political momentum that powers ever greater federal spending. The view of federalism in the 1930s undoubtedly served as a catalyst in the depression era, but growth has been sustained since that time by the raw political forces unlocked during that period. Because federal programs have been driven forward by these political dynamics, and not primarily by political philosophy, a conservative administration, with the backing of a conservative electorate, has been thwarted in its attempts to reverse the tide.

How Programs Begin

Government programs generally begin in one of two ways. They may be enacted in response to a perceived crisis or threat to society. Such crises accounted for the inception of many major spending programs including Social Security and the Aeronautics and Space Agency (NASA). Or the programs may start simply as small research activities or offshoots of existing programs. Either way, the result tends to be the same: Each program sets in motion a coalition of political forces that seeks to expand the program and to defend it from attack.

Perceptions of crises have been critical to the establishment of major new federal programs. As political scientist James Q. Wilson puts it;

> The most important new policies of government are accepted only after there has been a change in opinion or a new perception of old arrangements sufficient to place on the public agenda what had once been a private relationship, and to clothe a particular program with legitimacy. Organized groups can rarely accomplish such changes in opinion or such redefinitions of what constitutes legitimate public action; instead these changes are the result of dramatic or critical events (a depression, a war, a national scandal), extraordinary political leadership, the rise of new political elites, and the accumulated impact of ideas via the mass media of communication.[8]

The Great Depression provided the crisis and thus an opportunity to enact sweeping changes in the role of the federal government—changes that formed the foundation for what has been half a century of government expansion. Although extensive national social insurance programs had been enacted in some European countries, such as Bismarck's Germany, well before the 1930s, discussion of nationwide programs in the United States had been largely confined to academic circles. For the most part, there was confidence in America that the states, aided by a robust free-enterprise system, were well-equipped to deal with any foreseeable social or economic problem.

The breadlines and business contraction of the 1930s shattered that belief and undermined confidence in America's decentralized system of government. Those who advocated a strong national government, based on the liberal view of federalism, seemed to offer an alternative with real hope. This gave rise to a decisive shift in the political balance within the country, leading to the economic and social programs of the New Deal.

Similar crises ushered in other significant programs. The Soviet Union's launching of Sputnik in 1957, for instance, constituted a direct challenge to America's technological prowess and military security. It provided the stimulus for President Kennedy's successful request for congressional funds to establish the space program. Similarly, the racial confrontations of the early 1960s highlighted the jarring fact that racism and poverty coexisted in America with general prosperity. The upheaval helped to alter public opinion in a manner that made possible President Johnson's civil rights and Great Society legislation.

There is no particular reason, of course, to suppose that this process has ceased. Potential crises continue to loom large, and there is every reason to believe that some turn of events will lead to the creation of yet other major federal programs. The rapid rise in the cost of health care combined with an aging population, for instance, could well break the back of political opposition to a national health service in America—a proposal that so far has failed to win majority support in Congress.

When new programs begin as a result of perceived crises, the political balance changes decisively. Eventually, political and philosophical debates that preceded the new program generally fade away. Once programs such as Social Security or highway grants are set in motion, or new departments are created, the discussion soon shifts toward details such as the level of the budget and the proper scope of the new program. No longer is the existence of the program or agency at issue.

There are two principal reasons for this. The first is simply that once a critical decision is made, and the political blood has been shed, the administration and Congress are understandably reluctant for some time to reopen old wounds. Yet this does not explain why programs and departments go on to expand, generally remaining impregnable to attack, even many years after they have fulfilled their original purpose or acquired a record of waste and inefficiency.

The reason why they tend to continue despite criticism leveled against them, acquiring almost a life of their own, is that programs and departments become an integral part of the political process. Their very existence alters the dynamics of that process, shifting the balance of advantage into the hands of groups wishing to see more powerful central government and greater federal spending. The failure to comprehend this process fully and to devise a strategy to counter it explains the Reagan administration's complete inability to achieve more than modest victories in its budget battles as well as its failure to achieve its goal of a decisive reduction in the size of the federal government.

The Public Spending Coalitions

When spending programs are established, those who pay for them are almost never the same people who obtain the benefits, and only rarely is the average cost burden on the taxpayer equal to the average benefit obtained by the consumer of the service. This is very different from the competitive private marketplace, where there is a built-in tendency for the cost of a product or service to be borne by its consumers, and where consumers part with their money only when they feel that the value of their purchase is at least equal to its price. This critical difference between the two sectors leads to a supply and allocation of government services very unlike that in the private sector, and to peculiar political pressures tending to inflate that supply.

Political scientist James Q. Wilson distinguishes four ways in which burdens and benefits are distributed in the public sector. Each has slightly different implications for the dynamics of budget growth.[9] In one type of program, says Wilson, both the costs and the benefits are distributed over a large number of individuals. Social Security, interstate highway spending, mass-transit subsidies, and national defense and welfare programs are examples of such programs. In a democratic society, Wilson points out, legislators always have an incentive to raise spending on programs of this nature—even if there is little or no lobbying pressure—because the number of beneficiaries is so large.

A second group of programs benefit a small population and the costs are spread over most or all taxpayers, yet no well-defined interest group is especially burdened or hurt by these programs.

Such programs include agriculture price supports, the Rural Electrification Administration, "jobs" bills, Amtrak, and the whole host of pork-barrel spending bills that sail through Congress every year.

Programs of this nature form the backbone of "creeping" federal spending. They are fertile ground for pressure groups and lobbyists, who work assiduously to win support for spending in the full knowledge that they cannot afford a head-to-head confrontation between beneficiaries and taxpayers. In an open political contest, those who shoulder the cost of the projects would easily outnumber those who gain.

The third category identified by Wilson includes those programs that provide widely distributed benefits at the expense of a well-defined but smaller group. The politics of Medicare, says Wilson, differ from those of Social Security in that doctors are forced to shoulder paperwork burdens associated with the program. Pollution requirements on smokestack industries are another example. For the most part, these programs impose costs on segments of the population through regulatory requirements, not through taxation. Unlike the affected groups in the first or second kinds of programs, the groups burdened by this type of program have a strong incentive to resist expansion of the program because they bear most of the cost.

The final category of programs consists of those whose costs and benefits are both distributed among well-defined and relatively small groups. The National Labor Relations Board and the various trade-protectionist laws are examples of federal activities that pit the lobbyists of opposing interest groups against one another. Again, the costs and benefits of these programs stem generally from the regulatory activities of the federal government, not from its taxing and spending functions.

If we limit our discussion to those federal programs that spend money raised through taxes, charges, or borrowing, we can see that most budgeted federal programs fall into the first two categories identified by Wilson—that is, programs in which both the costs and the benefits are distributed widely throughout the population, or those whose costs are spread thinly and widely while the benefits are concentrated. The problem for the would-be budget cutter is that powerful coalitions develop around these classes of programs, making political action difficult.

Four distinct groups have a distinct interest in the preservation or expansion of such federal programs:

Beneficiaries and Near-Beneficiaries Whenever a new spending program is launched, a specified category of people becomes eligible for benefits under the law. But whenever a new program is debated before Congress, there is also pressure on legislators to keep funding near to the minimum necessary to serve this category. This pressure comes from fiscal conservatives and from those who fear that money might otherwise have to be withdrawn from other programs they support. The result is very often a conviction among the beneficiaries of the new program that the spending authorization is insufficient to meet their needs. It is common for people to feel that however much money government provides for a program to assist them, it is not enough. Beneficiaries, therefore, generally have strong motives to campaign for an expansion in the funding level.

In addition to those who benefit directly from the program, there is another group—one might call them "near-beneficiaries"—who do not quite meet the eligibility criteria of the original law and its regulations and yet, they believe, fit the intent of the law. This group has a strong incentive to press for modifications to the criteria to have themselves included under the program, through a change in the law, an administrative ruling, or a court decision in their favor—a method that has become common in recent years.

When a program has a budgeted spending limit, the near-beneficiaries and beneficiaries may well have clashing interests. A city that is pressing to extend the use of development grants to middle-class neighborhoods, for instance, can pose a challenge to another city that uses funds in low-income neighborhoods. After the pie is cut, in other words, the cost of redefining a program to help near-beneficiaries pits them against existing beneficiaries. In entitlement programs, however, total spending is budgeted but not limited by a fixed appropriation or directly controllable by any agency. Outlays depend only on the number of eligible people who demand services. In such programs the near-beneficiaries pose no threat to the existing beneficiaries and will usually seek the latter's support in pressing their claims. Although the existing beneficiaries may have nothing to gain directly from joining forces with the newcomers, they do have an incentive to see the group of beneficiaries widened, since the larger the number of beneficiaries, the greater is the political pressure that can be applied to expand the program—to the advantage of all beneficiaries.

Even with limited discretionary programs, it should not be assumed that there will be no cooperation between existing and near-beneficiaries. Those currently drawing benefits, for instance, may feel that the new group will enhance the public image of the program's beneficiaries, making future campaigns for a general increase in funding more likely to succeed. Or the demands of the near-beneficiaries may simply provide an opportunity for existing recipients to press their own case for more adequate funding, and by pooling their political forces both groups will gain.

Service Providers The second group with an interest in new programs consists of the private-sector individuals and businesses that actually supply the services. When roads are built to serve the community, construction firms, construction workers, and materials suppliers have plenty of opportunity for gain. When funds are made available to provide housing for the poor, house-building firms do not go unrewarded. And when programs are enacted to train the handicapped, to help juvenile offenders, or to improve adoption services, a corps of human-service professionals can look forward to more secure careers.

The potential service providers, then, have a clear financial interest in seeing a program started and expanded. If their industry already caters to federal programs, and thus has established a congressional lobbying arm, the service providers are usually far more potent and vocal campaigners for a program than are the direct beneficiaries themselves. Naturally, few service lobbyists are so crass as to emphasize the advantages to their industry that would flow from the new or expanded program. Defense contractors are careful to stress our endangered national security when they take out full-page advertisements urging Congress to buy more tanks and airplanes, and teachers are quick to argue at hearings that more funding and higher salaries are needed for science teachers simply to equip the nation with better technicians and engineers. Nobody, it seems, is out for his or her own interests.

Beneficiaries and private sector providers, then, are natural partners in campaigns for higher federal spending. For the beneficiaries and near-beneficiaries, the organizational abilities and lobbying power of professional groups or industries are welcome resources in the political battle. And for the service providers, promoting the interests of a group or purpose enjoying public sympathy takes attention away from the fact that they are also promoting their own interests.

Administrators Public-sector administrators of federal programs have a similar incentive to join the expansionist coalition. Like private-sector service providers, government bureaucrats have good reasons to push for an increased role for the federal government. Career bureaucrats have a natural desire to see departments or agencies grow, so that opportunities for their own advancement will develop, and political appointees often believe that public purposes are best served by an active government. Whichever reason applies to any individual official, it is logical for that person to aid the other elements of the coalition. As we shall see, this can be done in a number of ways.

Political Activists   In addition to elements of the coalition who have financial or direct career reasons for advocating the creation and expansion of programs, another group can be counted on to support the coalition's objectives, even if the individuals cannot be said to have a pecuniary interest in doing so.

This final element of the coalition is less easily defined. Indeed, there is often considerable debate regarding who can reasonably be included. But it is clear that certain classes of people—even though they are not directly involved in particular programs—have a philosophical or political reason for assisting the other elements of the coalition.

Many elected politicians are members of this fourth group, in that they enter politics to expand the role of the federal government (even though they may be elected at lower levels) to deal with what they perceive to be a need. Less charitable observers of the political process, of course, often argue that political office has a distinct financial value and that politicians provide benefits to their constituents in order to secure reelection and benefits for themselves. But even if we assume lofty ideals, we shall see that the political process tends to reward those politicians who vote for increased federal spending, and penalize those who oppose it.

A second group that fits within the political-activist category is the multitude of research and policy institutes engaged in public-policy debate. Some of these, such as those created by Ralph Nader, are explicitly described by their supporters as "public-interest" organizations. In general, they are openly political in their purpose, putting forward research data to support demands for greater federal regulation and spending. But they claim to have no pecuniary interest in such political action and to be interested only in helping the public cause as they interpret it. Other organizations in this category are less overtly political in nature. These include think tanks, university research centers, and scholars who share the liberal philosophy, together with institutes that simply wish to promote the interests of disadvantaged groups through research and information.

The public-interest groups in particular seem to attract proponents of greater federal activity. Surveys by Robert Lichter and Stanley Rothman, for instance, found that 90% of the leaders of the public-interest legal, research, and lobbying organizations based in Washington and New York consider themselves liberal. Since 1968, no Republican presidential candidate has received more than 4% of the votes of these activists, Ralph Nader and

Edward Kennedy head their list of approved public figures, each with a 93% favorable rating. Ronald Reagan managed a 5% approval score—one-sixth that awarded to Fidel Castro.[10]

Whatever the particular purposes and views of such organizations, they are critical to the political dynamics of budget growth by virtue of their research and lobbying. This can be said less emphatically, however, about another group that many feel is also influential in the campaign for a more active federal government—the media.

According to surveys by Lichter and Rothman, leading journalists with the most influential national news media display a strong commitment to the philosophy and economics of liberalism—television news reporters and producers being the most liberal.[11] Journalists respond, of course, that their political leanings are irrelevant; they are not like political activists because they have a professional duty to present information in a dispassionate way. Whether or not liberal journalists do act in this way—or can do so, given their perspective on the world—is a matter of intense controversy. Conservatives cite the editorial positions and news selections of *The Washington Post*, *The New York Times*, and the television networks as clear proof that these journalists consistently present a picture favoring an expanded federal role. And Lichter and Rothman feel that there is "at least some evidence that the perspectives of journalists do, in fact, influence the manner in which they perceive the 'news' and report it."[12] Whatever conclusion is reached on the influence of the media, however, one thing is clear: Both proponents and opponents of federal programs believe that favorable treatment in the media is critical to their success.

How Coalitions Cause Programs To Grow

When major new spending programs are debated before Congress, a face-to-face confrontation between opposing philosophies and interest groups invariably occurs. Programs such as Social Security, Medicare, each new weapons systems, general revenue sharing, and the national health system all led to set-piece battles that raged through the media and often became major election issues. In such well-publicized trials of political strength, heightened public discussion of the issues involved can often lead to the defeat of new programs, because the electorate is made aware of potential tax costs of a new program as well as its anticipated benefits.

Yet the contest is still by no means equal. The opponents of a new program must defeat it every time it is presented. Proponents of the program can come back again and again, hoping that a change in the political balance in Congress will tip the scales in their direction, or that some perceived crisis will provide them with an opportunity to stampede legislators into favorable action. And once it is enacted, the coalition benefiting from the program and its expansion begins to dig in, making the future dismemberment of the program steadily less likely.

As scholars of the "public-choice" school point out, the narrow coalition benefiting from a new program will tend to have the upper hand in subsequent campaigns to expand the program's scope and spending levels, even though it may be a small group compared with the number of taxpayers who foot the bill. The reason for this is that the coalition has much to gain from any expansion of a program, since the benefits are concentrated upon it. On the other hand, the costs are spread thin over the taxpayer population. A $100-million addition in spending for a federal road project, for instance, may mean substantial contracts for a few construction companies and easier commuting for a few thousand motorists. Yet it will cost the average taxpayer less than a dollar a year in taxes.

The beneficiaries of the spending can thus be expected to campaign hard for the project. It is rational for them to spend large amounts of money to secure passage of the necessary legislation or administrative decision, given their anticipated gain. But the cost imposed on any individual taxpayer is so small that he or she has very little motivation to take the lead—or even to follow another's lead—in opposing the program.

The imbalance of support for spending programs has become even more pronounced as previously local programs have been shifted to the federal level—and as the costs have come to be distributed nationally. When the supporters of a new road or new school have to appeal to city or county voters for funds, they are dealing with a relatively small number of people who are likely to have some first-hand knowledge of the issues involved. These taxpayers will look hard at the project or program before allowing the local government to dig deep into their pockets.

When essentially local projects are financed at the state level, however, voter resistance to proposed spending programs tends to be reduced, because the average burden on taxpayers is lower and because voters have to rely more on second-hand information (probably generated in the main by proponents of the program) and less on first-hand knowledge.

When a program is funded at the national level, this effect is even stronger. The costs are spread even thinner, and the typical taxpayer has to rely completely on second- and third-hand information. Consequently, the efforts of the public spending coalition can be concentrated on cultivating a favorable image of the project and of its likely effectiveness in solving the problem. This makes research and media coverage critical to the acceptance or rejection of new programs and the retention of existing ones. The acceptance in the 1930s of the idea that national approaches should be taken to problems that were once thought to be state and local responsibilities thus has had important ramifications for the political dynamics of budget growth.

This balance of interest has important implications for congressional politics. The coalition supporting a particular project or program expansion has an incentive to identify and lobby the key legislators on the relevant committees. If the potential benefits are considerable, the coalition may finance election campaigns against congressmen either to achieve the election of a more favorable legislator or simply to put pressure on the legislator. And even if direct political influence of this nature is not brought to bear, the congressman has to remember one simple fact of political life: You will hear a great deal from people in your district who want a special benefit, and on election day they will remember if you turn them down; but you hear little from constituents who might pay a dollar or two less in taxes because you turned down that special-interest plea.

If opponents of government expansion merely had to contend with an imbalance of electoral politics, their task would be difficult enough. But they face an additional problem once a program or department is created, because the coalition supporting it then has many additional opportunities to generate support for higher spending. It is often thought, for instance, that the federal administrators of programs are passive observers of the political process, even if they do have an interest in seeing their departments expand. Yet this is far from the truth, and such bureaucratic empire-building helps the coalition enormously. Bureaucrats have considerable power to promote the interest of the coalition of which they are a part, and they exercise it.

One of the indirect ways they do this is by awarding contracts and research grants. Laws are enacted that state the objectives of a program and the way in which money is to be spent, but it is the bureaucrats who promulgate detailed regulations and choose contractors. Hence they are in a position to strengthen those organizations that press for an expansion in the role and budget of the department. And they can ensure, at least to an important degree, that less supportive organizations are denied federal funding.

This power is particularly important in the area of research and information. By selecting topics for research, and by funding particular organizations to undertake that research, administrators can use federal money to produce data that tend to favor the expansion of programs. Such research is especially useful in identifying near beneficiaries who might be drawn into the coalition.

This is not to say, of course, that the federal agencies can determine the entire research on any topic. Universities, think tanks, and other private organizations produce independent information on programs. Nevertheless, federal departments are in a comparatively powerful position. They can time the publication of their research findings to coincide with their own proposals to modify the law; they can finance research by outside organizations to give "independent" support to their own bureaucratic objectives; and they can ensure that a supply of information is available to proponents of federal spending. In short, they can provide other elements of the coalition with the research ammunition and money they need to undertake a political campaign.

The relationship between a government department and the beneficiaries of its programs helps to cement together the coalition and to give it more political power. James Q. Wilson notes that this "bureaucratic clientelism" has been a characteristic of the growth of government in America and that it has followed a now familiar pattern.

> A subsidy was provided, because it was either popular or unnoticed, to a group that was powerfully benefitted and had few or disorganized opponents; the beneficiaries were organized to supervise the administration and ensure the funding of the program; the law authorizing the program, first passed because it seemed the right thing to do, was left intact or even expanded because politically it became the only thing to do.[13]

Wilson points out that interest groups have understood throughout the life of the Republic that the creation of new government departments is important to furthering their cause. The most recent example of this was the campaign to establish a federal Department of Education. But the process is well established.

> The formation of the Department of Agriculture in 1862 was to become a model, for better or worse, for later political campaigns for government recognition. A private association representing an interest—in this case the United States Agricultural Society—was formed. It made every president from Fillmore to Lincoln an honorary member, it enrolled key

congressmen, and it began to lobby for a new department. The precedent was followed by labor groups, especially the Knights of Labor, to secure creation in 1888 of a Department of Labor. It was broadened in 1903 to be a Department of Commerce and Labor, but 10 years later, at the insistence of the American Federation of Labor, the parts were separated and the two departments we now know were formed.[14]

These bureaucrat-client coalitions can be highly effective vehicles for extending programs in order to pursue the various goals of the staff and beneficiaries. In her analysis of policymaking in the Social Security Administration (SSA), for instance, Martha Derthick quotes Robert J. Myers, the SSA's chief actuary for many years, to the effect that the growth of Social Security benefits was encouraged by the SSA's staff—not because their primary purpose was to improve the lot of the beneficiaries, but because of the desire of public officials to enlarge their domain. Myers wrote in 1970:

> Over the years, most of the . . . staff engaged in program planning and policy development have had the philosophy—carried out with almost a religious zeal—that what counts above all is the expansion of the program. To some of them, to believe otherwise would amount virtually to being opposed to the program. Thus, such persons have not necessarily tended to be partisan as between the political parties, but rather they have favored and helped those who want to expand the program the most—it is only natural for people to advocate and work strongly for the growth of the activity in which they are engaged.[15]

According to Derthick, "the prevailing technique" at the SSA was to identify a social problem, such as a lack of health care, and then to devise a solution to that problem within the framework of a national social insurance system. The research department at SSA provided data and arguments to support such extensions of the Social Security System. SSA officials, says Derthick, allied themselves with organized labor in promoting mutually beneficial proposals. Organized labor, for instance, supported SSA proposals within the Social Security advisory councils and lobbied for them before Congress. The unions also financed public campaigns for extensions of social insurance, such as the inclusion of medical coverage, and founded the National Council of Senior Citizens, which lobbied hard in behalf of near-beneficiaries and program extensions. "Perhaps most important of all," writes Derthick,

Labor was an unofficial outlet for proposals that SSA officials were not free to promote themselves because they lacked approval from political superiors .... Organized labor and the SSA were, instead, intimate collaborators. There was little bargaining between them, little give-and-take over social insurance. Rather, there was a bond of sympathy, of shared commitment to social insurance as the chosen instrument of social welfare, and a shared antipathy to the program's real and putative enemies on the right.[16]

In addition to aiding the beneficiaries and near beneficiaries of programs in their quest to expand federal spending, administrators can also help strengthen another key element in the coalition—service providers. As mentioned earlier, the awarding of service contracts is one way in which this can be done. Such federal contracts have been a key element in the build-up of support for increased federal spending among private-sector providers of human services. Research by the Urban Institute demonstrates just how dependent the private nonprofit sector has become on direct and indirect revenue from the federal government. Data for 1980 show that 58% of total revenues to social service organizations came ultimately from the federal government. Community development organizations derived 43% of their revenues from federal sources, and nonprofit health-care agencies derived 22%.[17]

The importance of federal funding to the revenues of nonprofit community-based organizations has important implications for their goals, says Carl Milofsky, formerly of the Program on Nonprofit Organizations at Yale University. "Traditional community organizations tend to be crisis-oriented," he notes, and they draw support primarily from volunteers. The growth of federal human service programs, however, has had profound consequences for these organizations.

> During the last decade of government grantsmanship and expanded service delivery, the most common approach to the problem of insuring continuity and competence [among community organizations] has been the hiring of professional staff to take responsibility for continuous operations. While the goals of hiring paid staff may initially be quite limited, the creation of a staff bureaucracy inevitably adds a new self-perpetuating dynamic of growth and continuity to the affairs of community organizations. People work in bureaucracies because they expect to get paid. Since their livelihood depends on employment with the organization, they have a strong incentive to make the organization larger and more

stable in the interest of preserving their own jobs over the long term.[18]

Such professional service providers have few economic incentives to find ways of dealing with the problems of society in a less costly manner—by using volunteers, for example—and every incentive to press for those problems to be tackled by professionals with public money. Moreover, argues Robert Woodson of the National Center for Neighborhood Enterprise, these service professionals work with bureaucrats and politicians to obtain regulations, licensing requirements, and mandatory credentialing that crowd out nonprofessional, less expensive providers. Human-service professionals, according to Woodson, act like any other group of professionals or businessmen: They try to erect legislated barriers to entry against lower-cost alternatives. The result, he says, is higher-than-necessary spending channeled through providers who in turn campaign to raise costs and spending levels.

Legal action and media coverage can also be used to strengthen coalitions wishing to increase federal spending. So-called public-interest law firms and other organizations, in cooperation with beneficiaries and service providers, have made extensive use of the courts in recent years to force spending increases when the government is reluctant to authorize funds for certain purposes. In some legal cases, civil rights arguments and similar appeals have been used to convince courts to require government departments to extend benefits to a group of near beneficiaries "unfairly" denied them under a law or regulation. Even more common, however, is the use of legal action—even unsuccessful suits—to highlight the alleged shortcomings of existing programs and to win public sympathy for campaigns to add new spending. Favorable media coverage for such campaigns can also help to exert pressure on officials and legislators to agree to program extensions.

The Importance of Gradualism

Coalitions of this nature play an active role in set-piece national debates over major new program initiatives. But in widely publicized confrontations the opposition to increased spending is often better organized and more effective politically. When faced with a large increase in spending, contained in a clearly defined new program, the average taxpayers and their representatives may balk if the tax cost is heavy and the benefits are concentrated. Proponents of a 1943 bill, for instance, failed dismally in their attempt to enact a major expansion of social insurance that would have increased cash benefits significantly and added programs to provide disability insurance, health care for the whole population, maternity benefits, and federal unemployment compensation. But when this same bill was subsequently broken up and its elements considered separately over many years, "with individual pieces tailored to fit political circumstances of the moment," as Derthick puts it, much of the unsuccessful bill eventually became law.[19]

When measures are pushed forward in small stages, the advantage shifts toward the coalition that will benefit from the program, and away from the taxpayers. Given that the electoral balance is against them, skilled proponents of new spending avoid provoking the taxpayers by trying to obtain too much at once. They use the resources and power of the coalition, drawing on its ability to undertake research, fund lobbyists, and undermine alternatives to government solutions, to win public sympathy—or at least avoid overwhelming public opposition—in order to win small political victories. But each victory extends and strengthens the coalition, enabling it to press forward with further spending initiatives. The strategist who is proficient in the technique of gradualism will achieve everything that would be rejected if it were presented in a single bill.

This gradualist approach has proven highly effective in enabling interest groups to gain increases in federal spending, despite the general antipathy of Americans to the growth of government. According to Robert Myers, the technique has become the hallmark of campaigns to expand social insurance programs.

> The expansionists, as a matter of strategy, frequently use the "ratchet" approach. They do not unveil their ultimate goals in their entirety, but rather advocate only part. Then they are satisfied, for the time being, when they get only a fraction of that part. They believe that there is always another day to push forward their goals, and they know that once a certain expansion has been achieved, a retreat from it is virtually impossible . . . usually the ink is scarcely dry on a newly-enacted amendment before plans are being developed for the next legislative effort.[20]

Why Programs Cannot Be Cut: The Federal Ratchet

A ratchet allows motion in only one direction, and the ratchet strategy adopted by the proponents of federal spending is no different.

Although some cutbacks can be achieved, the resistance is usually fierce—typically far stronger and more determined than is the opposition to program expansion. The net result is a long-run tendency for government to grow, despite the efforts of even the most conservative politicians to contain it.

Just as electoral dynamics and political techniques available to the spending coalition generate the momentum for spending growth, so these same forces conspire to thwart attempts to cut spending. Since the costs of most government programs are distributed widely, and because the benefits are relatively concentrated, taxpayers are likely to see little more remaining in their pockets at tax time because a particular program has been cut or eliminated. On the other hand, the coalition benefiting from the program has much to lose if spending is reduced and so has every incentive to mount an expensive lobbying and public-relations campaign to persuade politicians and the public that the program is essential and a good value for the money.

Politicians on key congressional committees and the officials brought before them at hearings know well that an angry coalition can do their careers great damage, and they also know that average taxpayers are hardly likely to pledge their undying support just because they might one day have their taxes cut by a few cents. So there is always pressure on politicians to mouth platitudes about efficiency and fat-cutting while continuing to support specific spending programs that benefit powerful constituencies.

This is not to say that there are no occasions when the balance seems to shift, at least for a time, in favor of those who wish to see spending reduced. This may happen when gross fraud or mismanagement is uncovered in a program, or when a sudden rise in a program's costs forces a major tax increase, which is rare at the federal level because of the scale of the sector and its tax base. It may also happen when a politician manages to mobilize latent taxpayer irritation with ever increasing spending and direct it against the spending coalitions—as Ronald Reagan did in 1980 and 1981. But although these "taxpayer revolts" may achieve some initial successes, they rarely lead to lasting cutbacks. The reason is that the underlying dynamics still do not change. Such campaigns, James Q. Wilson observes,

> [are] rarely successful because the same force-a sudden adverse change—that stimulated the formation of the anticost group will lead to the formation of a pro-benefit group should politicians try to cut the budget sharply. Most office holders, knowing that they cannot really reduce the education or welfare budget by any significant amount without

precipitating an organized counter attack, rarely try very seriously to do so. Meanwhile, the anticost organization will attempt to minimize the threat it poses to the potential opposition by concentrating its fire on some budget item that can be plausibly described as a "frill." Though this may help neutralize the opposition, it rarely leads to large savings.[21]

Once again, it should be noted that this effect is more pronounced when taxing and spending take place at the federal level than when they occur at the local or state level. When costs are spread nationally, they are also spread thin. This makes it harder to initiate and maintain a national taxpayer revolt. Many states also have legislative and constitutional mechanisms that taxpayer groups can employ to lock in taxing or spending limits—often by referenda, such as Proposition 13 in California or Proposition 2½ in Massachusetts. This makes it easier to keep spending controls in operation after taxpayer anger dies down. Although constitutional constraints theoretically are available to the national taxpayer, however, they are far more difficult to trigger. Moreover, state or local taxpayers are less likely than national taxpayers to be bamboozled by cuts that are more show than substance. Just as national taxpayers have to rely much more on second- and third-hand information when they evaluate new spending proposals, they must also use such indirect information when evaluating the pain inflicted by spending reductions. And spending coalitions are quick to maintain that even the mildest cuts cause terrible hardship for the most deserving beneficiaries.

Campaigns to convince the public that spending reductions are extremely damaging to deserving people have been particularly problematic for the Reagan administration. Despite evidence to the contrary, the general impression among the public is that many major programs and departments were cut to the bone or eliminated between 1981 and 1984. This perception has, as one might expect, been strongly encouraged by coalitions of program supporters who wish taxpayers to believe that spending cuts have gone too far and that "essential" programs need to be reinstated. The success these coalitions had in portraying the Reagan administration's record in this way led to the steady evaporation of the momentum for budget reductions. Despite David Stockman's efforts to sweep away what he has called the "social pork barrel," crumbling congressional and public support prevented him from doing much more than chip away at the edges.

To resist campaigns to reduce federal outlays a spending coalition can utilize the same techniques that enable it to win increases in spending. The symbiotic working relationship among bureaucrats, beneficiaries, service providers, and public-interest organizations usually enables those groups to direct an effective counterattack against would-be budget cutters.

Research can often be deployed very effectively to blunt an attack on programs. After the shock of David Stockman's 1981 extensive "hit list" had worn off, for instance, a barrage of studies appeared from research and public-interest organizations. These studies criticized the proposed cuts and alternative policies put forward by the Reagan White House. Analyses from a host of organizations charged that cutbacks in social welfare and urban assistance would hurt this group or that. And when the Reagan administration argued in 1981 that many such federal programs should be replaced with help from the voluntary sector, the Urban Institute, in behalf of the charitable sector, quickly brought out two studies maintaining not only that charities could not be expected to make up "the gap" but also that the tax and spending reductions would reduce the resources of the nonprofit sector (thanks to tax disincentives and service-contract cutbacks) by $45 billion over four years.[22]

The Reagan administration had the authority, of course, to generate departmental studies and demonstrate projects to support its position. But political appointees within the various departments soon discovered that this was easier said than done. Professionals within government departments had little incentive to facilitate studies and proposals calling for a reduction in their responsibilities, and so made it difficult for Republican officials to accomplish their goal of changing direction.

The procedure used by professional staff to evaluate grants also enabled bureaucrats to undermine administration attempts to utilize alternative research institutions. Since government officials had been directing money toward a relatively small constituency of researchers and service providers, career staff found it easy to fault alternative organizations as "inexperienced" because they had no track record of working with the federal government. Political appointees who refuse to accept such "professional" evaluations can soon find themselves in hot water.

The Department of Health and Human Services discovered this when the secretary's office attempted to circumvent pressures from in-house staff regarding a 1982 discretionary grant program for economic development. Reagan officials brought in outside evaluators broadly favorable to the objectives of the administration to balance the professional staff. All the department managed to do, however, was to provoke angry denunciations in the media from the evaluators usually employed for the purpose. The administration was accused of ignoring the sound advice of experienced professionals and trying to channel money to organizations with no experience of government work. Rather than face a long-drawn-out dispute, Reagan officials backed off and generally overruled the recommendations of their own chosen evaluators, accepting instead the views of the professional staff.

This subtle but effective pressure from bureaucrats has helped to maintain the flow of research and contract grants to what some conservatives have labeled "the usual suspects," and thus reduce the ability of the Reagan administration to provide Congress and the public with research data favorable to its position.

The media also provide an effective instrument by means of which opponents of budget cuts can engender public sympathy for their position. When a reduction proposal is put forward, it is not difficult for critics to find a beneficiary who will be hard hit by the change. It makes little difference if the proposal can be amended to deal with the unintended effects of changes in eligibility criteria; the extreme case is grist to the media mill, and critics use it to characterize the entire cutback as unreasonable or inhumane. The Reagan budget cutters have been badly mauled in this way. Whenever they put forward a budget change, front-page stories carry the anguished testimony of a veteran cut from the disability-assistance rolls or of a senior citizen whose welfare check has been suspended.

Even when an administration survives such damaging campaigns and induces Congress to enact budget cuts, the results are often less dramatic than one would expect. The reason for this is that the budget process itself is no friend to the budget cutter. Initial spending "ceilings" passed by Congress are not binding upon that legislative body, and the authorization and appropriation process gives interest groups plenty of chances to breach the ceilings as the process continues. Victories won at heavy political cost during early deliberations of Congress can disappear entirely by the end of the budget cycle.

Management Improvements

David Stockman's inability to win more than an occasional round in the budget fight led some Reagan administration officials to maintain that important cost-saving improvements could be made in the operation of many federal programs, even if the scope of the programs themselves could not be altered. Several government departments claim that significant successes have been achieved in such efficiency drives.

It is unlikely, however, that these efficiency improvements are as extensive as officials maintain. And in any case, their impact is likely to warrant little more than a minor footnote in any account of government spending trends. Not only are such management reforms generally insignificant in the context of total federal spending, but there is also little reason to suppose that they will have any lasting effect.

Government departments simply do not operate under the same constraints as do private companies. Their revenues do not depend on the willingness of consumers to pay for their product or service. Nor do the twin pressures of competition and the profit motive force them to seek ever greater efficiency and threaten to put them out of business if they fail to do so. In a government bureaucracy, steady budget expansion and career advancement by seniority are more usual determinants of management policy. A determination to improve efficiency is a purely internal feature of such a bureaucracy, contingent upon the goals of a particular administrator—not an external imperative that the bureaucracy cannot ignore. Consequently, efficiency improvements rarely outlast their advocates. Once an appointee leaves the government, or simply becomes frustrated and tired, inefficiency begins to creep back into the department.

Because of these bureaucratic dynamics, the potential for savings of the kind recommended by the so-called Grace Commission is unfortunately very limited. The President's Private Sector Survey on Cost Control, under the chairmanship of J. Peter Grace, used private-business techniques to identify $424 billion in savings that could be achieved within the federal government, over three years, without any fundamental changes in policy.[23] The commission put forward very rational proposals for closing unnecessary military bases, amending overgenerous federal retirement, improving federal purchasing procedures, and many other sensible reforms.

Unfortunately, the commission could provide little guidance, given its mission, as to how the political dynamics might be altered to enable its proposals to be implemented. But without such a strategy, there seems little prospect that Congress and the civil service will do anything more than pay lip service to the report, and continue with procedures that fit the existing political and bureaucratic dynamics.

The spending coalition has shown itself well able to withstand siege by the Reagan administration. The new departments of

Energy and Education, created by the Carter administration, ai still standing despite Reagan's 1980 pledge to abolish them, and the trend of total federal spending has been little affected by the Reagan years. Some domestic cuts have been achieved, but most programs remain intact, albeit squeezed—ready to expand again as soon as political conditions become favorable. Meanwhile, defense spending has edged up to a new plateau.

The failure of the Reagan administration to reverse the growth of federal spending is highly significant. It marks the failure of the traditional conservative approach to budget cutting. This strategy rests on the premise that it is possible to mobilize and focus the anger of the majority of taxpayers, direct it against Congress, and force the passage of legislation to reduce the supply of taxpayers' dollars to those who clamor for federal spending. This supply-side budget strategy needs a president with strong leadership abilities, it requires a determination to act quickly and decisively, and it must have a well-thought-out laundry list of program cuts. The Reagan administration came to Washington with all those requirements, but it still could not cut the budget.

As we have seen, the inability of the Reagan administration to cut spending stems from the fact that nothing has been done to weaken the coalitions that drive federal spending, and thus to alter the underlying political dynamics that give these coalitions their immense political power. By not addressing these dynamics, the administration's strategy has proven to be fatally flawed, and its supporters have been easily outmaneuvered in the budget war of attrition.

If the administration is to halt the seemingly inexorable growth of government in America, it must abandon its purely supply-side approach to budget cutting. It will still be useful to continue pressing for sweeping budget cuts, if only to keep the spending coalition guessing, and program cuts should be implemented whenever the dynamics favor them. But that approach will do little by itself to shrink the size of government. Needed instead is a strategy designed to address the *demand side* of the political equation—to tackle at source, in other words, the combination of forces that causes Congress to create new programs and to expand their funding. If the administration can manage this, it might begin, at last, to dismantle the federal ratchet.

2

THE LOGIC OF PRIVATIZATION

The failure of the Reagan administration to cut federal spending does not mean that Reagan strategists have been unaware of the underlying dynamics of budget growth. But it is fair to say that there has been little evidence of creativity in the search for solutions to the impasse—for ways to dismantle the federal ratchet.

For the most part, conservative politicians have continued to look solely at supply-side mechanisms. They have sought, for example, the election of more legislators committed to the philosophy of small government, in the hope that these legislators would ignore constituency pressure to "bring home the bacon" and vote instead for spending reductions. They have also urged President Reagan to appoint tougher administrators to government positions—people who would not catch "Potomac Fever" and begin to exhibit the traditional characteristics of bureaucrats—so that agencies can be brought under control. And they have looked at legislative and constitutional devices, such as the line-item veto and the balanced budget amendment, to hold down total spending. The general approach can be characterized very simply: Change the personnel who legislate and administer spending programs, and place constitutional constraints on the operations of government.

So far, this strategy has not been a roaring success. There is little indication that the balance within Congress has been changed fundamentally; the great majority of legislators are still highly sensitive to electoral pressures favoring the spending coalition. Potomac Fever may not have reached epidemic proportions among Reagan appointees, but it is certainly widespread. Many die-hard conservatives who came to Washington intending to decimate the federal government seem to have found all manner of tactical reasons to preserve programs they once denounced. But even if things had been different, if, say, a highly motivated band of officials and legislators had consistently put philosophy above practical politics, there is little reason to suppose that the effect would have been permanent. To be successful over the long haul, such legislators would have to be elected year after year, and officials have to combine incorruptible ideological purity with administrative dexterity. In reality, one electoral reversal can sweep away all the gains made by such people, and can reopen the spending floodgates. And if legislators choose to ignore the interests of their most determined constituents, that electoral reversal is rarely long in coming.

The constitutional route, on the other hand, does hold the promise of a lasting solution to the problem, and so it is certainly worth pursuing. But it should be considered a longshot possibility. It would be folly to place all hopes for controlling federal spending in the amendment vehicle. Not only are the prospects for the passage in the Congress of such controls still highly questionable, but amendments have to be ratified by three-quarters of the states. As the backers of the Equal Rights Amendment discovered to their cost, that process can be a political mine field. Even though ERA swept through the Congress with ease, skillful campaigning by its opponents doomed it at the state level. Even if a spending-limitation amendment managed to pass the Congress, it would almost certainly face the same kind of political trench warfare at the state level. The spending coalition simply has too much to lose to allow such a measure to be passed. And even if it survived the long journey to final enactment, it would be subject to interpretation by the courts, like every other amendment. It is difficult to see how a spending limitation amendment, containing provisions dealing with emergencies and other special arrangements, could ever be made immune to tampering by the judiciary.

Mrs. Thatcher Shows the Way

The Reagan administration has yet to experiment with a public spending strategy that takes account of these political facts of life. In this regard it is well behind the Conservative government of Margaret Thatcher. Coming to power in Britain in 1979, Mrs. Thatcher, like Ronald Reagan, faced a steadily growing public sector. Thatcher also faced an economy dominated by government-owned (nationalized) heavy industry and basic services. Unlike Ronald Reagan, however, Thatcher began to employ a technique—

known as privatization—that has enabled her government to make remarkable gains in her battle to cut the public sector down to size.

Public spending and government ownership took a quantum leap in Britain with the Labour party's victory in the 1945 general election. Within five years, the government of Clement Attlee had created the National Health Service, established a comprehensive welfare state, and nationalized key segments of British industry—"the commanding heights of the economy," as the Labourites put it.

Attempts by later Conservative governments to roll back the socialist revolution of 1945 were notable only by their lack of success. The British people demonstrated a marked unwillingness to give up their "free" medical treatment, despite the inevitable shortages that plague the taxpayer-financed National Health Service. And the nationalized industries have proved far more difficult to shift back into the private sector than most had expected. To some extent this has been due to the threat of renationalization under future Labour governments. But more important is the fact that the industries became less and less commercial the longer they remained in public hands. This made it very difficult to attract private buyers. Once the incentive to make a profit was removed, thanks to government subsidies, the industries ceased to make a profit. Public ownership did not bring with it the virtue of firms operated for the good of citizens rather than stockholders. Instead, management decisions merely began to reflect narrow political considerations. New and uneconomic steel plants were located in swing districts, utility prices were kept artificially low, and railroad connections were maintained without regard to profitability. Perhaps most important of all, nationalized industries came to be viewed as a means of keeping down unemployment through overstaffing, adding to their inefficiency and enormous losses.

Faced with the cost of these public enterprises and the difficulty of moving them into the private sector, government after government attempted to bring financial discipline to the nationalized industries. The 1970–74 Conservative government of Edward Heath, for instance, asked teams of private-sector managers and accountants to recommend efficiency improvements (much like the Grace Commission in the U.S.), and in several instances even to take over the operation of government programs and firms. But as Madsen Pirie of London's Adam Smith Institute explains, such initiatives have proved disappointing because public-sector operations cannot be made efficient. There is simply no incentive structure forcing the sector to become competitive and profitable. Efficiency drives, says Pirie, may cause paper clips to be reused

and an occasional limousine to disappear, but there
lasting improvement.

> The effort is commendable, but of temporary
> campaigns have achieved limited success, but
> the period of pressure. When the novelty has die
> tices of public supply gradually reassert their c....... The
> history of the public sector in Britain is littered with the
> names of "whiz kids" who wrought beneficial but short-lived
> influence from the private sector.[1]

Similarly disappointing results accompanied another strategy
adopted by British governments—the imposition of "cash limits" on
government departments and nationalized industries. Advocates
of this approach, like American proponents of rigid spending limits in the federal budget, sought to force bureaucrats to cut out
unnecessary spending by making departments compete, like
private concerns, for the limited available funds.

The problem, writes Pirie, is that spending limits give departments no incentive to become more efficient, only a requirement
that they spend less. So the programs and expenditures retained
by a department do not reflect necessity; they reflect only the
interests of the bureaucrats. Instead of cutting their own jobs and
salaries, administrators tend to trim services to the least powerful.
In order to undermine the entire cash-limit campaign, bureaucrats
often propose cutting services to those who can be expected to
react strongly against such cuts.

> Those who oppose limits on spending know which are the
> most popular and sensitive areas of service; these are the
> ones put at risk first. Savings in the welfare program can
> only be achieved, it seems, by closing schools for handi-
> capped children and throwing dependent old people out
> onto the street. Naturally enough, the media coverage of
> these horror stories begins long before they happen, ably
> assisted by leaked memorandums showing more atrocities on
> the way. Government [supporters in Parliament] wilt under
> the hail of fire, and the cash limit campaign has its fangs
> pulled.[2]

Officials in the Reagan administration would no doubt find this
phenomenon all too familiar.

The search for ways to turn back the state in Thatcher's Britain
did not, however, stop at efficiency drives and attempts to impose
cash limits. Instead, the Thatcher government learned from the
deficiencies of these approaches and adopted a new strategy

esigned to bring marketplace pressures to bear on government departments in a very direct way. If public bureaucracies cannot cut costs and operate efficiently simply *because* they are public bodies, the Thatcherites reasoned, then they must be moved into the private sector; they must, said Thatcher, be privatized. By so doing, the inherently inefficient dynamics of a publicly operated program or firm would be replaced with the consumer-oriented dynamics of a private venture.

On the face of it, the privatization strategy adopted by the Thatcher government seems to differ little from the largely unsuccessful attempts of previous Conservative governments in Britain to denationalize state-owned firms (that is, sell them to the private sector). But although the end purpose may be the same, the technique employed has been very different.

Previous approaches to denationalization consisted of straightforward attempts to sell off government-owned ventures essentially "as is" to private buyers. So a potential buyer had to face the prospect of a firm hamstrung by inefficiency, misallocated resources, overstaffing, rigid and unproductive work practices, and (usually) heavy losses. In all probability the prospective buyer would also acquire a hostile work force and would risk the possibility of renationalization in the future. As a consequence, governments rarely faced a stampede of buyers.

The privatization strategy adopted by Margaret Thatcher, however, has sought to bring market forces into the picture in several different and less direct ways:

- *Contracting out* public services to private-sector firms, so that the government continues to finance the service, but private-sector firms are invited to bid for the contract. In this way, competition and private sector efficiency replace bureaucratic incentives.

- *Deregulating* statutory monopolies and licensing barriers that prevent private-sector firms from competing for customers with government-owned firms. This approach has been used to stimulate the creation of private firms to take over functions now handled by government, and to encourage state-owned firms to improve their procedures, so as to make them more attractive to private buyers.

- *Denationalization,* or the sale of publicly owned firms or assets. The Thatcher government has given two new twists to the traditional approach. Deregulation has been used, as mentioned, to make previously unsalable enterprises more attractive to buyers by forcing the companies to compete. But more important, the government has used creative methods to transfer functions into the private sector, to neutralize the opposition, and to discourage renationalization.

Tables 2 and 3 provide an overview of the extent of the privatization through sale of publicly owned corporations, as of mid-1984, together with the principal future targets the government has set itself. Within 10 years of Margaret Thatcher's assumption of office, the government expects to have disposed of public assets worth about £9 billion (equivalent, as a proportion of GNP, to sales of $100 billion in the U.S.).

Yet these figures do not reveal the full extent of privatization in Britain, nor do they demonstrate the range of techniques employed. The Adam Smith Institute, Britain's leading center of research on this subject, has recorded twenty-three different methods of privatization, each involving subtle variations of the three principal methods described earlier. These techniques have been used not only to sell government shares of companies but also to contract out many local government services and parts of the National Health Service; to foster private alternatives to government; and to entrench privatization through sales of firms. Some examples are of particular note.

Sales to Small Investors and Employees

In an effort to prevent the later renationalization of a privatized firm, the Thatcher government has sought on occasion to encourage ownership by its workers and by small investors, on the assumption that it will be hard for a future socialist government to take back a firm in the name of "the people" if the ordinary people of Britain already own it. For example, when a majority holding in the North Sea oil exploration company, Britoil, was sold to the public in 1982, special preference was given to applicants requesting small numbers of shares. A bonus of extra shares was made available to small shareholders if they held their stock for at least three years. When the share issue was tendered, 99% of applications came from small investors, and 92% of the eligible employees of Britoil purchased stock.

The government used a similar approach when it sold the National Freight Corporation to its staff in 1981. Like many nationalized companies, National Freight had a long record of losses and poor labor practices and seemed an unlikely candidate for denationalization. So the government negotiated an employee buy-out, and 82% of the stock was turned over to more than half of the firm's 21,000 employees, their families, and former employ-

Table 2
Privatization since Margaret Thatcher Took Office

Company	Date	Method	Yield (in millions of pounds)
BP (British Petroleum)	Nov. 1974 and Sept. 1983	Government holding reduced from 51% to 31%	817
ICL (computers)	Dec. 1979	Sale of government's 25% holding	37
Fairey (aerospace)	May 1980	Sale by stock offering	22
Ferranti (electronics)	July 1980	Sale of government's 51% holding	55
British Aerospace	Feb. 1981	Government holding reduced from 100% to 49%	43
British Sugar Corporation	July 1981	Sale of government's 24% holding	44
National Freight Corporation (trucking)	Oct. 1981	Sale to management and staff	5
Cable and Wireless	Nov. 1981 Dec. 1983	Government holding reduced from 100% to 23%	443
Amersham (chemicals)	Feb. 1982	Sale by stock offering	65
Britoil	Nov. 1982	Government holding reduced from 100% to 49%	627
British Rail Hotels	Nov. 1982	Sale to private companies	51
Associated British Ports	Feb. 1983 April 1984	Sale by stock offering	96
International Aeradio (communications)	March 1983	Sale to Standard Telephone and Cable	60
British Gas Corporation (oil assets only)	May 1984	Sale to private bidders	82
Enterprise Oil (North Sea gas)	June 1984	Sale by stock offering	380
Sealink (English Channel ferries)	July 1984	Sale to British Ferries	66
Inmos (microchips)	July 1984	Sale of government's 75% holding	95
Jaguar (cars)	Aug. 1984	Sale by stock offering	297
British Telecom (telephone system)	Nov. 1984	Sale of 51% by stock offering	3,900
			£7,185 million

Table 3

Planned Privatization

1985	Privatized shares (%)	Anticipated yield (in millions of pounds)
British Airways	100	500
British Airports	100	400
Beyond 1985		
National Bus company		100
Land Rover (vehicles)		100
Unipart (British Leyland auto parts)		50
British Nuclear Fuels		300
Ordnance factories		300
Naval shipyards		100
Rolls Royce (aerospace)		100
		£1,950

ees. The remaining 18% was acquired by four banks. The buy-out has been an enormous success. Inefficient work rules were soon ended, and the company quickly began to show handsome profits. Within two years of the sale, the employee-owned shares had quadrupled in value.[3] There seems little chance that a Labour government could ever take back such a worker-owned firm into public ownership.

In 1984, the government completed a $250-million marketing campaign to encourage the widest possible sale of British Telecom, the nation's telephone system. The year-end sale was by far the largest stock offering ever in Britain or the United States and involved an all-out advertising blitz to persuade ordinary Britons to "share in British Telecom's future." Central to this campaign was the offer of a $20 voucher against future telephone bills to anyone buying at least $300 worth of shares. The aim of the strategy was very clear: Make sure that the privatized British Telecom is owned by millions of Britons, so that renationalization is impossible.

eight buyout enabled the Thatcher government to
that would normally oppose denationalization—
isting work force—into strong advocates of private
Conservatives achieved the same result with their
public housing to sitting tenants. Approximately
families were living in subsidized government-
owned units, and such public housing constituted a considerable
drain on the Treasury—as well as a major political headache for
Conservative governments. Whenever officials tried to raise rents
enough to cover costs, they could expect a solid block vote for
antigovernment parties. There appeared to be no method available to break up the powerful self-interest constituency committed
to below-cost public housing.

But the Thatcher government found such a method: Make
tenants an offer they cannot refuse by enabling them to become
the owners of their housing units. Instead of trying to pursue an
unsuccessful and politically damaging campaign to raise rents, the
Conservatives recognized that they could never hope to recoup the
cost of operating housing by extracting higher rents from the
tenants. So they gave the tenants the right to buy their units at
discounts of up to 50% of market value. In this way, the government eliminated costly operating subsidies on each unit sold,
obtained an immediate infusion of cash, and turned dependent
tenants into independent owners.

The program has been a phenomenal success. More than
500,000 units have been sold to tenants since 1979, and Conservative candidates in the 1983 general election reported dramatic
changes of political support among former public-housing tenants
who had purchased their dwellings. In just four years, the
Thatcher government managed to turn part of a key constituency
supporting government spending on housing into a powerful
source of support for private ownership, low taxes, and smaller
government.

Contracting Out

Although private garbage collection is widespread in the U.S., it
was practically unknown in Britain until 1980, when Southend-
on-Sea hired a private company to provide service. Since then,
scores of local governments have begun to contract out a variety of
services, with significant savings to the taxpayer. More recently,
private contractors have provided nonmedical services for the
National Health Service and even maintenance work for the Royal
Air Force.

The significant aspect of the growth of contracting out in Britain, however, is not the range of services involved, but the way in which the campaign developed. Public-sector service workers are highly unionized, and they normally act as a strong brake on any moves by politicians to improve efficiency or to utilize private-sector alternatives. But in the matter of local government contracting out, it was private-sector service companies, not politicians, who promoted privatization. Once Exclusive Cleaning, Ltd. had demonstrated major savings in Southend, for, instance, it embarked on an aggressive national campaign to market private-sector garbage pickup. The company placed full-page advertisements in local papers, guaranteeing property-tax savings, thanks to cost reductions, in what turned out to be a highly successful effort to win voter support for privatization—and thus put pressure on local politicians. Most important, Exclusive managed to neutralize opposition from unionized public-sector workers. In many instances, the firm offered to hire public employees to work on its private contracts with increased pay and better conditions. It followed this up with an advertising campaign aimed directly at other public-sector workers, featuring folksy interviews with former city workers who had joined Exclusive—interviews that stressed improved pay, better worker-employer relations, and cleaner equipment.

The company-based campaign was very effective in reducing worker opposition to contracting out. It also welded together a coalition of employees, companies, and taxpayers who became a potent force for spreading sympathy toward privatization. In short, it created a powerful interest-group lobby, driven by profits, better wages, and lower taxes, that successfully overcame the seemingly impregnable lobby for public-sector service provision.

Incentives to Countergroups

The British government, understanding the importance of establishing counterconstituencies in furthering privatization, has begun to aid this process by offering carefully crafted incentives to key segments of the population. The discounted sale price for public-housing tenants quickly built up such a constituency. But an even more interesting example, in many respects, concerns health insurance.

Despite failings that are obvious to any visitor from overseas, the British National Health Service (NHS) is as close to the heart of the average Briton as apple pie is to the heart of the typical American. No politician would dare suggest that it be dismantled or replaced. And so the system continues to provide free but inadequate care to rich and poor alike. While maintaining a firm commitment to health service, however, the Thatcher government has begun detaching key groups of supporters from the NHS and creating a coalition designed to move at least part of the nation's health care into the private sector.

Before the Thatcher government took office, private health insurance was utilized by less than 10% of the population—generally highly paid executives. One reason for this was that in Britain, unlike the U.S., group-health insurance premiums were not tax deductible, and so those who wished private hospital care were forced, in practice, to pay both for NHS coverage and private insurance. The Thatcherites changed this law. Now company-based group-health premiums are fully deductible for any employee earning less than approximately $12,000 per annum.

After the legislation passed, the predictable constituency began to form. Blue collar workers have flocked to private health care, so that it is no longer the prerogative of the rich, and the health-insurance industry has grown rapidly—with many traditional insurance companies branching out into health care. Suddenly a powerful, widely based coalition of beneficiaries and service providers has appeared in Britain, and it is pressing for more private health care. The government has accomplished this not by attacking the sacred institution but by *diverting* public support from it.

Deregulating Monopolies

The Thatcher government has used deregulation, as well as targeted incentives to stimulate private-sector alternatives to monopoly government services, thereby inducing the pressure of competition to force efficiency onto the public sector. Licensing restrictions have been eased on long-distance bus service, for instance, to open the door for private competitors to the state-owned British Rail and the nationalized intercity bus company. The move has led to the formation of several low-cost "no-frills" services, as well as luxury bus companies that offer "in-coach" video films and microwaved meals.

The most important demonstration so far of deregulation as a device to foster privatization, however, concerns the Post Office. In pre-Thatcher Britain, the Post Office also operated the telephone monopoly. The 1981 British Telecommunications Act ended the partnership by splitting the Post Office into a postal service and a telecommunications division—renamed British Telecom (BT). In addition, the act licensed a new network, Mercury, to compete with BT, and licensed private firms to supply telephone equipment directly to customers. The act also deprived the Post Office of its monopoly over express-mail services and the delivery of Christmas cards.

The deregulation of the telephone monopoly led to an explosion in the use of new services and equipment by telephone users. As with health care, telephone deregulation proved to be the catalyst for the creation of a new coalition—comprising telephone manufacturers, service providers, and users—that is now urging further deregulation and privatization. This coalition has forced the government to move much faster and further with the denationalization of British Telecom than even Mrs. Thatcher had intended.

Vouchers

A voucher provides a cash-equivalent subsidy to an individual who can use it to purchase specific goods and services in the open market. Food stamps in the U.S. are an example of such vouchers. From the privatizers' perspective, the voucher is a useful device to make private-sector alternatives financially available to low-income citizens. Since vouchers subsidize individual demand, not supply, it is not necessary to provide a heavily subsidized service for all citizens. The subsidy can be restricted to the target population.

The British have begun to use vouchers to enable certain groups to buy adequate transportation services. Tokens in various denominations are distributed to eligible people, such as the handicapped and elderly, and the carrier later redeems the tokens. So far, the vouchers are limited to use on public transportation, but a campaign is under way to allow eligible people to use the tokens to purchase rides from private minibus and taxicab services.

Constructing a Private-Sector Ratchet

Recent British experience provides valuable guidance as to how privatization could be used as a general strategy to cut government spending in the United States. The technique has worked well in Britain because it attacks the political dynamics that cause government to grow and become entrenched. Privatization replaces this set of dynamics with another that discourages citizens from demanding public-sector services and encourages them instead to seek similar services from the private sector.

Unlike the supply-side approach to budget reform, which is usually thwarted in the long run by public spending coalitions, privatization adopts a demand-side approach. The supply-side approach forces politicians to deny government services to consumers, thereby inviting hostility from both providers and consumers of those services. The demand-side approach, however, allows politicians to offer more attractive private services while forcing nobody to accept them. By concentrating on the circumstances that cause people to demand government spending, and by altering those circumstances, the demand-side approach tackles the budget problem in a totally different way from that used by most conservatives, including Ronald Reagan. Madsen Pirie speaks of "micropolitics," which he sees as the essence of the privatization approach.

> Micropolitics is the art of generating circumstances in which individuals will be motivated to prefer and embrace the alternative private supply, and in which people will make decisions individually whose cumulative effect will be to bring about the desired state of affairs as the product of voluntary actions. The process of transfer from the public to the private economy is most securely achieved when its progress is evolutionary, arising from free decisions.[4]

The experience of the Thatcher government suggests that privatization is an effective method of changing the political dynamics that favor increased public spending. The British experience also indicates that if the strategy is to be successful in reducing the size of the federal government in America, it must be founded on four key general principles and tactics:

1. Establish the government as the facilitator, not the provider, vider, of goods and services

There is a popular but mistaken assumption, E. S. Savas points out, that because a society may decide that certain goods and services should be provided, government must provide them.[5] This does not follow. Services desired by a society can be provided by individuals, churches, voluntary associations, private companies, and a host of other institutions. Government services are merely one option.

Opponents of large government, however, often fall into the opposite trap. They argue that the only way to reduce spending on a service is to deny government any role in its delivery. In many instances, such as the multitude of minor pork-barrel projects initiated by Congress, they have a point and can count on public sympathy for their position. But when they apply the sweeping argument to programs such as Social Security, they destroy any chance there might have been to win public support for budget reductions.

The privatization strategy, however, does not necessarily deny a role for government in the provision of services. It simply gives government the role of *facilitator* rather than *provider* of services. The government may require services to be provided (such as mandating citizens to enroll in a retirement plan); it may encourage private provision (through tax incentives, for instance); or it may allow private provision (through deregulation)—but privatization starts from the assumption that government does not have to be the provider.

This is important in dealing with sensitive programs. The Thatcher government did not begin the privatization of the National Health Service by taking the politically suicidal position that government has no role in health care. Instead, Mrs. Thatcher has pledged that her government will make health care available to all, but that it will do so while encouraging those who can afford it to obtain care in the private sector. Similarly, no politician in America could expect to be elected after informing a group of senior citizens that the federal government had no role in the provisions of Social Security. On the other hand, as we shall see in Chapter 6, there would be great political potential in a proposal that tackled Social Security's financial crisis by requiring all citizens to enroll in a pension plan. The government would make a federal plan available, but would encourage Americans to seek a private alternative based on enhanced Individual Retirement Accounts.

2. *Divert demand into the private sector*

Encouraging people to demand services from the private sector, rather than from the public sector, is the heart of privatization. This combines political expediency with the objective of cutting federal spending. It allows politicians to gain points with constituencies by promising more, not less, and by giving people the freedom to choose the service provider most attractive to them. And by relieving the pressure of demand for government programs, it reduces the political opposition to budget cuts.

The key to doing this, of course, is to design policies that make the private alternative more attractive. This can be done in a number of ways: by altering the relative price through tax incentives, by imposing user charges on the publicly provided service, and by employing many other similar devices. Privatization does not mean that would-be budget cutters must require the private sector to charge full cost, while the government service remains grossly subsidized. They do not even have to provide a level gaming table. Given the objective of shrinking government, they can load the dice in favor of the private sector, just as the public spending coalitions have, for decades, managed to load them in favor of government programs.

3. Detach elements of the spending coalitions

Any military or political strategist knows that weakening the opponent is the first step to victory. The advocates of government growth understand this well, as explained in Chapter 1. They have used research, media campaigns, litigation, and many other devices very effectively to grind down the opposition to new government programs and to weaken those trying to eliminate existing ones.

A privatization strategy can be successful only if it, in turn, weakens the coalitions supporting spending programs. Devices to neutralize the opposition have been a common feature of privatization in Britain. Discounts to tenant buyers, for instance, weakened resistance to the sale of public housing; private garbage collectors "bought off" public-employee opposition to contracting out by hiring government workers; and turning employees into shareholders was remarkably successful in breaking down obstacles to denationalization.

American strategists should bear these examples carefully in mind. They should remember that a public-spending coalition usually comprises people and organizations that have very different motivations. There are generally many ways in which elements of the coalition can be detached, or even turned against each other, so that the power of the coalition is significantly reduced.

4. Create mirror image private sector coalitions

Just as the expansion of government has been driven by coalitions of beneficiaries and near-beneficiaries, service providers, administrators, and political activists, the contraction of government must be powered by similar coalitions in the private sector. Privatization involves the conscious creation of these coalitions.

The political dynamics of privatization coalitions are the mirror image of those of the public-spending coalitions. Privatization involves concentrating benefits on a limited segment of the population—beneficiaries and service providers—while the costs (assuming tax relief and other special privileges to one group mean costs to everyone else) are spread widely. Consequently, the privatization coalition is provided with a set of incentives to press for an expansion of the private-sector alternative, while those who bear the cost (if any) of the incentives have much less motivation to oppose expansion. Moreover, the near-beneficiaries of privatization—those who are not quite eligible for benefits under the current legislation—have an incentive to ally themselves with existing beneficiaries in order to press for wider availability of the private alternative. The privatization coalition can be expected to lobby strongly for a greater role for the private sector, and to generate research and media coverage to win support—just as its mirror image in the public sector lobbies for an increased role for government.

Coalitions do not arise and grow by accident. Spending coalitions gel around new expenditure programs. When their lobbying pays off in new spending, they become stronger politically and are thus able to demand further spending. They grow incrementally and cause programs to grow incrementally. Similarly, privatization coalitions gel around targeted tax incentives or regulatory changes, and successful lobbying for further benefits also makes them more powerful. Like their public-sector counterparts, these coalitions and their privatized services grow incrementally. But a comprehensive privatization strategy can aid this process. It can stimulate the creation of such coalitions and nurture them, in the knowledge that, once created, they will take on a momentum of their own.

It is also important to appreciate that coalitions will fight other coalitions that threaten their existence. Like an antibody in the body's immunity system, a privatization coalition is the natural enemy of a public-sector coalition. The reason for this is that if the goods and services required by a society are being provided through the public-sector, private channels for serving that demand are being ignored. In addition to campaigning for general public and political support, therefore, privatization coalitions can be expected to wrestle for influence with their mirror-image coalitions, weakening both the pressure for public spending growth and the resistance to budget reductions.

Founded on these four principles, the privatization strategy could become a potent weapon for achieving reductions in federal spending within the context of the American political system. By diverting demand for services into the private sector, and by weakening the coalitions seeking to preserve and expand the public sector, privatization makes the political contest more even. The strategy enables the budget cutters to acquire allies in the private sector and to pursue their goals in the context of reduced demand for government services, instead of facing a solid wall of opposition when they propose rational cuts in public spending. In other words, fewer people have less to lose from program reductions.

The enthusiasm with which the Thatcher government adopted the privatization approach, after decades of frustrated attempts by Conservative governments to contain the growth of the state, has been rewarded with dramatic successes at the national and local levels. In the United States the privatization process is advancing at the state and local levels—chiefly in response to budget pressures and mainly in the form of contracting out. The contracting out version has also been a feature of some federal programs (some of the problems related to that will be discussed later), but no administration to date has developed a comprehensive privatization strategy as a means of rolling back the growth of the federal government.

Implementing a privatization strategy in America would present special challenges. Admittedly, an American president would not face Mrs. Thatcher's institutional problem of grossly inefficient nationalized industries and seemingly implacable labor opposition. However, the Thatcherites have been able to use their solid parliamentary majority to ensure passage of carefully designed and timed legislation—a luxury denied to the White House. Moreover, the British parliamentary system has the virtue of being much less susceptible to special-interest pressure than is the U.S. Congress.

This means that in an American version of privatization, the task of building coalitions is even more important than it has been in Britain. Creating these coalitions, and weakening the public-sector coalitions, would have to be the top priority for a privatization strategy to succeed.

Varieties of Privatization

Government services come in many forms, and the privatization model has to be adapted to fit each variety. There is a big difference, for instance, between moving Amtrak into the private sector and trying to privatize welfare or defense.

E. S. Savas has examined the characteristics of government goods and services and the variants of privatization most appropriate for a comprehensive strategy.[6] Savas points out that two broad properties can be used to classify all goods and services: exclusion and joint consumption. Exclusion means that the potential consumer can be denied the good or service by the supplier; for example, a person can be denied or excluded from a public-housing unit. A joint-consumption good—as opposed to individual consumption—is one that can be consumed jointly by a number of people without diminishing the quantity or quality of the good—national defense, television broadcasts, or national parks, for instance.

Savas uses these two characteristics to place goods and services within a framework of four categories. In each instance the word "good" is used to denote either a good or a service.

Private goods exhibit properties of exclusion and individual consumption. These goods or services are consumed individually and cannot be obtained without the agreement of the supplier, usually contingent upon the payment of a price or fee. Most goods and services supplied in the private marketplace, such as automobiles and houses, fall into this category. Collective or government action normally plays little or no role in the supply of such goods. It is usually confined to providing laws for orderly markets, safety regulation, and the like.

Toll goods, on the other hand, are characterized by exclusion and joint consumption. These goods are used jointly, but payment can be extracted for their use, and individuals can be excluded. Such goods include roads, railroads, and sewer services.

The third category, *common-pool goods*, notes Savas, can be consumed individually; but exclusion is difficult or impossible, and so it is hard to levy a charge directly. The air and the open range are examples of such goods, as is the supply of fish in the sea. The difficulty of charging directly for common-pool goods in an equitable and efficient manner arises from the fact that the market does not ensure a supply to match the demand. As a result, a society tends to resort to collective or government action to provide or protect the goods.

The fourth category, *collective goods*, can be consumed only jointly, and exclusion is difficult. A national defense program, for instance, can provide protection only jointly. No individuals under its umbrella can be excluded from that protection if they refuse to pay for it—even if they do not want protection. Such goods and services present great problems to the marketplace. Individuals have every incentive to demand and consume collective goods until they are satisfied, without contributing to the cost—that is, they have a tendency to become what economists call "free riders."

Savas points out that the divisions between these classifications are by no means clear-cut. Even national defense is not a pure collective good, since some areas of a country, such as key industrial centers or missile silos, may well be given special protection. And some goods can be a combination of classifications. Protection for a factory or home, for instance, may involve the local police force (a collective good) combined with a supplemental security service or burglar alarm (a private good). Moreover, side effects, or externalities, can accompany private goods. Personal health care would normally be considered a private good, for instance, but it may carry important externalities with it if it reduces the spread of diseases. And garbage collection or a well-kept garden may affect only individual beneficiaries in a rural setting, but could be considered a toll or collective good in a large city.

The Role of Government

"Government," writes Savas, "can be viewed as nothing more than an instrument for making and enforcing decisions about collective goods."[7] But, he adds, there are several complicating aspects of this general statement, and they have important implications for the privatization strategy.

The first arises from the fact that there often is no consensus regarding which goods and services can be classified as common-pool or collective goods, and so there is also no agreement on the proper degree of government involvement in their supply and allocation. The tendency over the years, however, has been to reclassify goods toward the collective end of the category spectrum. To some extent this reflects a spreading belief that charges cannot or should not be levied for certain goods or services. Charging tolls at a bridge or fees for trash pickup, for instance, may be considered technically difficult, or not worth the management cost. And making each person pay the full cost of medical treatment or education is thought by some to be both impractical and immoral.

Also public-spending coalitions have a strong political reason for trying to reclassify goods and services as collective in nature, in order to justify spreading the cost over the general population. Affluent patrons of Washington's Kennedy Center Opera House, for example, can be counted on to wax eloquent about the externalities of good music and dance, for if the performing arts benefit the nation collectively, then patrons can reasonably argue that at least part of their evening's entertainment should be paid for by the taxpayer. Business supporters of energy research use a similar argument. Such research benefits everyone in the long run, they claim, and so it is proper to expect the taxpayer to pay part of the cost of expensive research and demonstration projects. Externalities, it seems, reach wider every year.

It is clearly in the interest of a public-spending coalition to devote resources to convincing the general public that goods and services the coalition desires have such externalities and collective characteristics. The more successful the coalition is in doing this, the more persuasive will be the argument that the costs should be spread through the tax system. If taxpayers feel they are gaining some indirect benefit, they will be less likely to oppose new spending or to favor cutting an existing program. Research organizations associated with spending coalitions, therefore, are eager to detect all manner of externalities associated with programs they wish to promote or protect.

The second complicating aspect of Savas's general statement about the role of government concerns the appropriate vehicle for delivering collective goods and services—assuming they are, in fact, collective in nature. He notes that there is a big difference between accepting that government is *an* instrument for ensuring the supply of a collective good and agreeing that it should be *the* instrument. Such goods can be delivered through many alternative organizations—and many different levels within a federal government. The voluntary association is one, as Tocqueville and others have observed. In the early days of the Republic, many a road, church, and school was built through collective action, and paid for collectively, without a hint of government support. Drawing on this history of nongovernment collective action in America, Peter Berger and Richard Neuhaus note that American society is rich with private organizations that address collective needs. These "mediating structures," as they call them, include family, church, neighborhood organizations, and a host of other formal and informal groups.[8]

Within formal government structures, moreover, collective goods can also be delivered at various levels; they do not have to emanate from Washington. As noted in Chapter 1, public-spending coalitions have an incentive to argue for government-provided goods and services to be financed and delivered at the national level, so that the cost is spread as thinly as possible. Coalitions frequently will use the externality argument to press their claim, maintaining that the benefits of what seems to be a targeted program are actually national in scope. So a bridge in Connecticut or a dam in Arizona, for instance, is said to be part of a *national* transportation or water system, not merely a benefit for nearby residents. In this way, collective goods and services that could be delivered quite adequately at the state or local level—assuming, of course, that taxpayers felt the expenditure was justified—are often provided via the national coffers, thereby tilting the political balance of advantage further toward those who wish to see increased government spending.

A third point noted by Savas is that even when there is complete agreement that the supply of a collective good should be organized and ensured by government, it does not follow that government has to provide that good directly. The government can act as the facilitator of a service. The federal government, for instance, could require health-insurance companies to enroll poor Americans without charge, or it could make funds available for private organizations to deliver services on behalf of government, as it now does. There are many ways in which government can make sure that a service is provided, without itself acting as the provider.

Reducing the Scope of Government

The economic and political characteristics of goods delineated by Savas require matching privatization techniques. Privatization, in effect, requires the reexamination and reclassification of goods currently provided by government, followed by the application of the most suitable method to transfer some or all of the government's responsibilities into the hands of the private sector.

Three principal privatization mechanisms are available. They are *load shedding*, where the government transfers the tasks of funding and providing the service into the private sector; *contracting out*, where government directly finances the supply of the service, but uses private sector suppliers; and *vouchers*, where the government provides consumers with the funds they need to purchase the service in the open market.

1. Load Shedding

In a strict sense, the only mechanism that could truly be called privatization would be load shedding, since this means ending the government's role completely as the provider of the service. Under load shedding, however, a government could still remain as the facilitator and regulator of the service. Load shedding is the primary approach being used by the Thatcher government in its policy of denationalization.

The most appropriate candidates for load shedding are private goods and toll goods, because charges can be applied to the consumers through a market mechanism. When the consumer cannot afford to pay the market price for a good to which society feels all individuals should have access (food, medical care, and shelter, for instance), a voucher would be more appropriate—although voluntary associations, perhaps encouraged with tax incentives to donors, might also be a suitable option.

It does not follow, of course, that a program transferred to the private sector would be delivered in the same quantity—or at all—by the private sector. Opponents of privatization no doubt would claim that this is true because the program is a collective good and the market therefore cannot function adequately. But the reason, instead, may be that it is actually a private good subsidized by taxpayers and that the beneficiaries simply do not value it enough to pay for it themselves. Obviously, the coalition benefiting from government provision has every incentive to discourage load shedding.

2. *Contracting Out*

Contracting out government activities means that the government retains its function as the funding source, but the good or service is supplied under contract by a private-sector firm or organization. The government, in this instance, chooses the quantity and type of service and pays the supplier. This method of privatization is most appropriate for common-pool or collective goods—where it is difficult or impossible to charge the consumer because of the exclusion problem. But it is also a possible approach when government needs to purchase private goods in order to deliver a collective good, such as defense.

Contracting out government services has become widespread at the state and local levels in the United States, and it is becoming more common in Britain. The Reason Foundation, based in California, maintains a data base of more than three hundred companies that provide services traditionally performed by government, and a 1982 federal survey discovered that one-third of all U.S. cities with populations above 2,500 contract out at least one service.[9] These services include fire protection, garbage collection, street maintenance, data processing, park maintenance, detention-center operation, and legal services. And cities report significant savings through contracting out. Although the practice arouses considerable opposition from public-sector unions,[10] the potential savings have made contracting out extremely attractive to financially strapped cities.

Contracting out has also grown steadily in importance at the federal level. But the federal experience has uncovered some of the dangers implicit in this type of privatization, as well as its potential.

Government functions contracted out at the federal level are as varied as those at the state and local levels. They include data processing, catering, health services, maintenance, cleaning, printing, security, research, transportation, and, of course, the development and production of major weapons systems. The principal vehicle for the contracting out of *commercial* goods and services required by the federal government (that is, standard private goods such as typewriters or trucks for the army) is circular A-76, issued by the Office of Management and Budget (OMB). The A-76 program, begun in 1955 and revised most recently in 1983, requires federal agencies to conduct cost comparisons between its internal suppliers and bidders from the private sector. The agency is then required to choose the most economical alternative. According to a survey of A-76 contracts, conducted by the Reagan administration,

> Circular A-76 has an impressive track record for generating substantial savings. Almost 1,700 cost studies have been conducted since 1979 resulting in an average savings of 20% over the previous cost of the commercial activity to the government—*regardless of whether federal employees or contractors won the competition.*[11] [emphasis added]

The most extensive use of an A-76 program, the study found, was in the Defense Department, where savings averaged 27% in situations where cost comparisons could be made. OMB calculates that throughout the government approximately $6 billion in annual federal outlays are used to purchase standard commercial goods and services covered in A-76. But it admits that this may be an undercount, since agencies have tended to focus only on "blue-collar" activities, overlooking potential savings in engineering, paralegal, and similar operations. If these were to be included, notes OMB, perhaps as much as $15 billion in annual outlays would become subject to A-76, with possible savings of $3 billion to the taxpayer.[12]

In addition to A-76 procedures covering commercial goods and services, many other functions of government are contracted out—although that term is generally not applied. The design and manufacture of weapons systems for the military, for example, is undertaken by private companies under contract. Lawyers in private practice provide legal services for the poor as part of a federally financed program. The federal government also pays private doctors and hospitals to treat patients under the Medicare and Medicaid programs, and most federal welfare services are delivered by privately owned service providers.

The experience of contracting out suggests that great care must be used in designing procedures for this type of privatization. One significant issue, relevant to the A-76 program, is the method used to conduct cost comparisons between government and private suppliers. Private contractors complain that the current method is rigged against them. Just to be considered, the private firm has to demonstrate savings of at least 10% in personnel-related costs, compared with the agency's estimate of its own costs. And the private company must present a firm fixed-price bid, which the agency then compares with an inhouse *estimate*. Moreover, private contractors, if they are to stay in business for long, must factor into their bids such items as federal, state, and local business taxes, fringe benefits, attributable overhead costs, insurance, and many other costs that do not appear in full in agency cost estimates.

Federal employees systematically try to shut private firms out of government contracts by hiding the true cost of the government option, according to many private companies. In addition, Congress, under pressure from public-employee unions, has passed measures limiting contracting out. The new exclusions on contracting out in the Defense Department serves as an example. Various other bills have been debated in Congress in recent years. They include measures placing tight restrictions on contracting out and legislation allowing public employees to seek court reviews of contracts.

Complaints about contracting out do not all come from the private-sector side, however. In the past few years, the media have carried many horror stories of contractors who raised their prices after an award was made, and of defense suppliers who charge hundreds of dollars for parts costing only a few cents at Sears. The implicit conclusion in these complaints is that such inefficiencies and profiteering would not occur if the function had been retained in-house. Yet this overlooks a simple point. Are we to believe that a Pentagon bureaucrat who blithely agrees to spend $400 for a hammer would suddenly apply Scrooge-like standards of scrutiny to work undertaken by his colleagues in government? Indeed, it is because costs must be itemized in the private sector that such bureaucratic inefficiencies come to light and can be corrected. With in-house suppliers, such outrages can go on for years without detection.

The clear lesson that can be learned from these cases is not that there is some inherent flaw in the private sector. It is that keen competition is a critical requirement for efficient contracting out. If a contractor can get the government to pay $400 for a hammer, he has every financial incentive to do so. The taxpayer must rely on the contractor's sense of honesty if he is to get value for his dollar. But if a competitor is watching over the firm's shoulder, ready to take away its government business, the contractor is under pressure to be as efficient as possible. In the Defense Department, of course, open competition is often difficult, because the need for secrecy and specialized technical skills limits the number of available suppliers for advanced weapons systems. But this is not a problem with most departments of government, and it is an exaggerated problem in Defense.

Just as competition is a critical requirement for effective privatization by contracting out, so budget savings cannot be expected if the government gives private suppliers a blank check for their services. This absurd policy has formed the basis of Medicare and . Medicaid programs for the elderly and the poor. Under these programs, the suppliers (physicians and hospitals) decide which services shall be provided and what prices shall be charged, and then they send the bill to the federal government, which pays it virtually without question. The economic incentives implicit in this method of contracting out are roughly analogous to those created by a rich father who telephones a car dealer to inform him that his son is coming to buy a car and that the dealer should give the son whichever car he wants and bill the father. It is unlikely that the son would return home with a used Volkswagen. Blank-check contracting out of medical services has had the same results. Fortunately, the Reagan administration took the first step toward eliminating these perverse incentives with its policy of paying fixed amounts for diagnostically related groups of procedures (DRGs). That change was a welcome move toward sanity in large-scale contracting out.

A final problem with contracting out concerns the public spending coalitions that drive up the federal budget. Private-sector service providers who are financed by government have a strong incentive to encourage Uncle Sam to spend more on the services or goods they provide. Weapons contractors can be counted on to lobby for more defense spending, and social-welfare experts for more social spending. Indeed, moving the supply function out of government may simply replace muted bureaucratic pressure for bigger programs with a well-financed private-sector campaign clamoring for more federal spending.

This significant drawback of contracting out means that it should be viewed with great caution as a means of privatization. The economic purpose of privatization is to reduce federal spending by moving functions out of government and into the competitive marketplace so that more efficient choices are made. But the political purpose is to reduce the power of the public spending coalitions. Load shedding accomplishes both purposes. Contracting out can certainly lead to more efficient government, but it does not guarantee smaller government. It is very much the second choice to load shedding.

3. Vouchers

A voucher is a government grant to an individual, to enable him or her to purchase specified goods or services in the marketplace.

Since a market must function for a voucher to be effective, it is suitable only for the purchase of private or toll goods. A voucher is normally provided to classes of citizens believed by the government to have insufficient income to pay the market price for a good or service. Normally a limit is placed on such a voucher (but it can always be supplemented with private funds), and it can be used only for a certain purpose. The idea is that the government provides the individual with the means to buy only a certain amount of a specific good, and so the consumer has the incentive to "shop around." Food stamps are an example of a voucher; so is the recently enacted housing voucher program, which helps poorer Americans to rent housing in the open market.

Vouchers have many advantages, but they also have some of the same deficiencies as contracting out. Their main advantage is that they allow a market to function in which the consumer—rather than the supplier or the government—is in control. From an efficiency point of view, this is very important. Because the recipients of vouchers have an incentive to choose the private supplier who meets their demands most closely and economically, the needs addressed by the voucher are likely to be met at the lowest cost to the taxpayer. And unnecessary spending is reduced because the assistance can be targeted only to those who need it, in contrast to a supply subsidy that brings the price down for everyone just to help a few (mass-transit subsidies, for instance).

The voucher also has attractive political implications for the privatization strategist. By removing the service provider as an integral part of the government-organized delivery system, it weakens the public-spending coalition. It does not eliminate the suppliers' incentive to back the coalition, but by stimulating competition among suppliers it does weaken the cohesiveness of the service-provider lobby.

Like contracting out, however, the provision of vouchers still means that segments of the private sector have an incentive to press for more government spending—in this case, the beneficiaries and near-beneficiaries. The privatizer must bear this carefully in mind when designing initiatives.

Fine Tuning the Strategy

It should be clear from the discussion so far that privatization is not a simple technique for cutting the federal budget. It does not have the elegance of a constitutional amendment or the romance of a plan centered on the persuasive powers of a charismatic leader. But unlike these approaches, it addresses the reality of the interest-group dynamics that drive the American political system. Indeed, privatization could be described as a strategy based on political guerrilla warfare.

For a guerrilla campaign to be successful, tactics must be adjusted to fit the terrain and the composition of the enemy. And no guerrilla campaign can succeed if it does not win over the support of the people. Similarly, the details of a privatization strategy must be adjusted to the politics and economics of each federal program. True collective goods have to be treated differently from private goods or toll goods: Load shedding might be the most attractive approach in principle, for instance, but in many situations a voucher may be far more practical from a political standpoint.

The techniques available to the privatizer are varied, and they can be used in combination to achieve the broad objectives of the strategy. These techniques are summarized in the following pages.

Improving the Political Environment

1.   Challenge the classification of goods

Proponents of a privatization campaign can point out that the benefits of a program are highly concentrated, and not spread over the entire population as its defenders maintain. Moreover, many federal services are actually a combination of the categories discussed earlier. The weather service, for instance, provides general weather information that may well be a collective good, but it also provides highly technical, specialized information for which there is a potential private market. Dividing services can allow the privatizers to concentrate on segments of the service rather than arousing public anger by attempting to privatize the whole service—or they can fashion different privatization techniques to deal with each aspect of the service.

2.   Press for programs to be administered and financed "closer to the people"

The more programs and their financing can be shifted to lower levels of government, the more they are likely to be challenged by taxpayers. President Reagan's New Federalism initiative sought to move in this direction. The White House proposed phasing out the federal government's responsibility for certain programs and transferring both the spending and taxing authority to the states. Although the administration attempted to sweeten the negotiations for mayors and governors by offering to take full federal responsibility of several basic social programs, the states understandably rejected the proposal. State and local officials well understood that there would be less support for in-state spending if state taxpayers, rather than national taxpayers, had to foot the bill—meaning there would be many angry beneficiaries and service suppliers come election time.

It is clearly not easy to persuade lower levels of government to accept full responsibility for programs, even if they are of purely local concern. Nevertheless, every success in shifting programs down the federal ladder makes it that much easier to control the size of federal spending—and every failure makes controlling the growth of government that much more difficult.

3. Develop a spending-taxing linkage in the minds of the people

Congressmen opposed to spending programs could attach specific financing mechanisms onto spending bills. This could help to build up opposition to the measures, because taxpayers would be able to link particular taxes with particular programs. The more those financing devices were concentrated on powerful lobbies, the stronger the opposition would be. Similarly, spending-reduction bills could be linked to tax relief for concentrated groups of taxpayers, in order to increase pressure for the cuts.

Weakening the Public Spending Coalition

4. Apply user charges whenever possible

The more the user of a service has to pay, the more attractive the private alternative becomes. When combined with a tax incentive for the private alternative (see 8, below), a user charge can be a strong incentive for consumers of federal services to switch their demand into the private sector. Increasing the price of the government service, moreover, alters the competitive position of private-sector suppliers and encourages the formation of private alternatives to government provision.

Some analysts include user charges as a version of privatization, but really they are not. Charges merely place part of the cost of a government service on those who use it. This is beneficial from the standpoint of equity and economy, but it does not mean that the service is transferred into the private sector. It is accurate to say, however, that applying user charges to services currently provided by government would encourage privatization by altering the relative prices of private and government suppliers.

5. "Buy out" key elements of the spending coalition

Different elements of a spending coalition often support programs for very different reasons. Giving some of those elements a stake in privatization can break up even the most powerful coalitions, as Margaret Thatcher discovered in Britain. By appreciating this, privatizers may be able to achieve success by making the private alternative particularly attractive to key supporters of a current federal program.

6. Fight the research and public-relations battle

It is often difficult for members of the public to rally around a private alternative to government if they are unfamiliar with it or suspicious of it. The Reagan administration failed to sell off its weather-service satellites, for instance, because no public debate on the merits of privatization preceded the announcement that they were for sale. The idea of selling the satellites seemed silly to the average American, and opposition grew steadily against the proposal. Demonstration projects and the release of favorable studies, however, can offset attacks on privatization initiatives—and they can be useful in identifying potential supporters. Similarly, critical analyses of studies generated by a spending coalition can put that coalition on the defensive.

Fostering Private-Sector Coalitions

7. Deregulate government monopolies

Ending government monopolies on the supply of goods and services, and eliminating restrictive licensing rules obtained by private providers of federal services, would encourage new private suppliers to form and to lobby. These new organizations could form the nucleus of coalitions to shift functions out of the government's hands.

8. Provide tax incentives to encourage privatization

Tax incentives are powerful instruments to foster the development of private-sector coalitions. They provide a concentrated benefit for those who choose the private-sector option, while spreading the "cost" (assuming other taxes have to be raised) across the entire taxpayer population. This gives the beneficiaries of the tax break a strong pecuniary interest in campaigning for increased privatization and in preserving services already privatized. The tax incentive is to the spread of privatization as the small new program is to the expansion of government spending. It is the catalyst or focus around which the mirror image coalition can grow, and it provides the concentrated economic benefit that drives that coalition.

Because tax incentives are so critical to the privatization process, it is important for supporters of privatization to be cautious in their support for tax simplification. Flat-tax and other tax-reform proposals could be dangerous for the privatization strategy because they usually call for the elimination of most deductions as a *quid pro quo* for a reduction in tax rates. It is hardly surprising that the proponents of such reforms include many politicians who also advocate a larger federal government, since denying tax relief to Americans who wish to choose private alternatives to government makes those alternatives less attractive.

9. Strengthen privatization coalitions

In addition to regulatory relief and tax assistance, there are other ways in which friendly politicians and administration officials can strengthen the political impact of a privatization coalition. One such method is funding research to locate potential beneficiaries and service providers and then binding them into a network. In the field of human services, for instance, many alternative private providers are not organized, and often they are overlooked by those who advocate greater reliance on the private sector. Officials can foster these providers by explicitly recognizing them as legitimate alternatives, by removing the red tape that excludes them from government contracts, and by including them in hearings and official commissions. Political legitimacy is a prerequisite for political power.

Supporters of a larger public sector have always understood the importance of organizing networks and advocacy coalitions. Those who oppose large government have tended to rely far too much on mass education to produce results. Privatization is a strategy that uses the coalition-group approach of the liberals to bring about a conservative goal.

10. Use incrementalist rather than revolutionary tactics

It was noted in Chapter 1 that there are occasions when public policy can be changed dramatically—generally as a result of some real or perceived crisis. But it was also noted that the success of the movement for major federal programs is due more often to the technique of creating small, inoffensive programs that become the focus of political campaigns to press for ever greater spending.

The privatization campaign should take the same approach. Occasions may well arise when a substantial reform of a federal program can be achieved. The most likely road to success, however, lies in the incrementalist approach. The privatizer should attempt to get a foot in the door with a regulatory change, a tax break, or a change in contracting procedures that will begin the process of coalition building. That coalition can be assisted and counted on to press for more changes to strengthen itself. In this way, the chances for substantial privatization in the future can be significantly improved.

The following chapters will apply this line of reasoning to a number of federal programs, arranged according to categories that have common characteristics and present similar challenges. The discussion is not intended to be a comprehensive, program-by-program agenda for cutting federal spending through privatization, however. The major spending areas, such as Social Security and welfare, will be examined in detail. Otherwise, programs will be selected that typify privatization solutions that might be applied more generally throughout the federal budget.

Privatization is not a panacea for the problem of escalating federal spending. And the idea of privatization does not rest on the contention that the federal government has no legitimate role as a direct provider of services. Privatization is suitable, however, for those goods and services that society believes should be provided, but for which federal provision is costly, inefficient, and subject to political dynamics that benefit undeserving groups. In these instances, privatization would reduce the demand pressure for federal programs, making cutbacks in spending far more possible.

3

FEDERAL ASSETS

The Importance of Ownership

Unlike the British government, the U.S. federal government does not own large segments of the manufacturing sector. It does own vast tracts of land, but it is not a principal owner of the steel plants, utilities, airlines, and the various other commercial enterprises that form the core of Margaret Thatcher's privatization drive.

Even though government-owned assets may not be as critical to U.S. public finances as they are in Britain, they do have a significant impact and important economic implications. Government ownership means, for instance, that certain of the nation's assets, such as public lands, are not being used productively because marketplace pressures do not apply. This may seem perfectly reasonable to a backpacker, but it implies that the government is denying itself considerable annual income or sales revenues, and also that it is bottling up resources that could bring more benefits to more people if utilized in a different way. What may appear, therefore, as a relatively small line item on the budget actually obscures an enormous cost to the government and the nation. This in turn means that funds are being denied to other programs and that taxes are being extracted unnecessarily from the taxpayer.

In reviewing the budget impact of federally owned assets, therefore, it is not sufficient to look simply at the annual budget item related to each asset. One must ask several questions. Why is the asset held at all if it imposes a cost on the government? If it is not a collective good, why should it not be sold to the private sector and charges levied on its users? And if the asset does have the characteristics of a collective good, would private management—or even some form of private ownership—allow it to be used by legitimate interests while generating income for the government?

As we shall see, such questions often reveal that what are supposedly federal assets are actually federal liabilities. And many assets owned and operated by the federal government "for the people" are in reality providing benefits of great value to a limited number of Americans.

To appreciate the potential impact of privatizing federal assets, it should be recognized that federal ownership and operation of assets are not like private ownership. The incentive structure is very different. In the private sector, competition and stockholder pressure force managers to seek methods of giving the consumer or client the maximum possible benefit at the lowest cost to the owner. In the bureaucratic public sector, managers behave very differently. Ownership is less concentrated and tangible, and so the owners—the general public—exert less pressure. Officials of the Bureau of Land Management, for instance, may have to report to a congressional committee on their latest acquisitions from time to time, but they do not have to face an annual meeting of angry stockholders who want to know why the company is losing money and their shares have dropped in value.

Similarly, public-sector managers are more open to special-interest pressures than are those in the private sector. Private companies invite bankruptcy if they put special interests before efficiency. But like other federal programs, federal assets tend to attract coalitions of interest groups whose goal is to benefit from a program financed by someone else (the taxpayers). The imbalance of pecuniary interests between beneficiaries and taxpayers, discussed in Chapter 1, combined with the political malleability of public-sector managers, generally ensures that government assets provide less than optimal benefits to the populations they were intended to serve, while placing an enormous burden on the taxpayer.

Privatization can improve the budget picture in such instances while enabling the asset to give more benefits to the public. It does so by altering the management incentives and by bringing stronger ownership pressures to bear on utilization decisions. This is not to say that simply selling off publicly owned assets is an appropriate policy. Selling off the Lincoln Memorial to the highest bidder might turn it into a profitable video game arcade and thus reduce the deficit by a few dollars. But clearly millions of Americans would be outraged by that change of ownership, even those who never intend to visit the monument. By contrast, vast tracts of federally owned land in the West are poorly managed and effectively closed to the public, while privately owned land in Maine is well managed, teeming with wildlife, and open to vacationers.

Privatization of federal assets does not mean selling off national treasures at knock-down prices to raise quick cash for the government, like selling the family silver to pay the servants. Nor does it mean allowing private-sector interests to exploit national assets and those who depend on them. It means using the private sector, where appropriate, to own or operate what are now federal assets in order to achieve public purposes at lower cost to the government—and thus to the taxpayer.

The notion of ownership is central to the idea of privatizing federal assets. Ownership provides people with a stake in an asset and encourages them to manage and use it as efficiently as they can. When people have no such stake, they tend to behave differently towards the asset. They may want more of it, because they bear no responsibility for the cost of upkeep, and they may waste it, because they have no particular reason to protect its value. And although national ownership technically means that every citizen has an equity interest in the asset, few people actually think of themselves as owners in any normal sense of the word. Privatization recognizes this. By investing true ownership of an asset in a group of people other than "the nation," the privatization strategy seeks to encourage that group to manage the asset more economically and more in accordance with the stated purposes of the program.

In some situations this may mean recognizing that so-called collective goods are in fact private goods, implying that the beneficiaries should carry the full cost of ownership and operation. In other instances it may mean contracting out asset management to the private sector to improve efficiency. And in yet other matters it may mean using the ownership principle to bring about behavioral changes that reduce the demand for a range of government-sponsored services.

Three programs will be examined in this chapter, together with the potential of the privatization strategy for improving their budgets. They are public housing, Amtrak, and federal lands. This is not, of course, a full list of federal assets, nor will everyone agree with the classification of these programs under the rubric of federal assets. They are chosen for two reasons. First, the privatization technique employed centers on aspects of each program that can best be described as assets. Other federal activities such as the Postal Service, defense, and air traffic control also involve federal assets. But the discussion of privatization in those matters will focus on the service function of those programs, and so they will be dealt with later as federal services. The second reason for the choice is that these programs illustrate well the variants of privatization that can be used to deal with other federal assets.

Public Housing

In the context of federal budget deficits approaching $200 billion, public housing expenditures may seem of minor importance. After all, the operating subsidies for approximately 1.2 million households runs at "only" $1.5 billion, and the budget authority for modernization is about $2 billion. Yet it serves as an example of a program where the federal government finances and maintains an asset which supposedly benefits one segment of the population (low-income Americans), but which, in fact, provides substantial rewards to other groups (construction firms and housing service companies, for example). And it does so while discouraging improvement within the very communities targeted for help. The importance of the privatization strategy for this and similar programs is that by changing the pattern of ownership of control, privatization serves to reduce both direct and external costs while improving the quality of assistance.

The Public Housing Problem

Public housing began in 1937 as part of the public works programs intended to stimulate the economy during the depression. In essence, the program consisted of the federal government providing principal and interest payments for bonds issued by local Public Housing Authorities (PHAs) to enable them to build apartments for lower-income families. Tenants were to make rental payments covering maintenance, utilities, and other operating costs. In other words, public housing was not seen at its inception as a means of housing welfare families. It was to erect improved housing for the temporary poor and for working families. But more important, it was intended to create jobs.

Since 1949, however, the program has been targeted more toward lower-income families. Until that time, rental income covered all operating costs and made a substantial contribution to capital costs. But since the Housing Act of 1949, rule changes and legislation have placed tight limits on the proportion of a tenant's income that can be taken in rent, and instituted requirements on PHAs to include more low-income families in the tenant population. By 1981, the rules specified that 95% of all new tenants and 90% of all current tenants had to be of very low income (no more than 50% of the area median family income).

These rent and tenant income requirements mean that subsidized public housing began to serve a needier group of beneficiaries, but they also necessitated further support from the federal government because rents were held low. Moreover, says housing analyst John Weicher, these modifications "removed the financial constraint on operating expenses that had effectively been imposed by the tenants' rental payments." Operating subsidies began in 1969 at $13 million, or a dollar per month per unit. By 1983 the subsidies had topped $1.3 billion, averaging $103 per unit per month.[1]

If the purpose of publicly funded housing is to accommodate low-income people who cannot find adequate shelter, then it might seem reasonable for the cost of the program to rise. Yet a closer examination indicates that the manner in which public housing is owned and managed has caused costs to rise unnecessarily, benefits to flow to people who are far from poor, and social conditions to deteriorate.

Public housing is remarkably expensive. The average construction cost is only a little below that of the price of a median new home, and various economic analyses put the cost of new units at about 25% more than comparable private housing.[2] One of the most important reasons for this is that the Davis-Bacon Act applies to federal construction projects. This legislation, passed in 1931 and heartily supported by organized labor, requires the "prevailing scale" obtained by local construction workers to be paid for federal work, and it sets specific limits on the proportion of skilled and unskilled workers who may be employed on federal projects. Similar rules apply to modernization work using funds from the $1.5 billion federal modernization program.

While changes in the Davis-Bacon rules put into place by the Reagan administration have somewhat reduced the impact of the law, the general effect is still to require the federal government to pay union rates and to use unionized construction companies. According to studies by the General Accounting Office and other institutions, the act has boosted construction costs by 5% to 10%. The high cost of building, modernizing, and operating public housing does not necessarily mean, therefore, that low-income public housing tenants live well at the taxpayers' expense. It does imply that the providers of public housing—construction companies and their employees—live well.

One of the great ironies of the nation's experience with public housing, moreover, is that the program's early proponents maintained that it would help to stabilize and restore the fabric of inner-city neighborhoods. But clearly that has not happened. Indeed, the deteriorating physical and social condition of many of the nation's public housing projects indicates that instead of stabilizing and improving communities, the program tends to destroy them.

The laws and regulations reward high-cost construction. And since the managers hired by the PHAs have little incentive to be sensitive to the needs of the tenants—or to those of the federal government, for that matter—there is little pressure on them to be efficient. Investigations of certain PHAs, such as the one in Chicago, have shown the authorities to be vehicles for all manner of corruption and cronyism.

The underlying flaw in public housing is that the incentive structure associated with its ownership and management arrangements rewards many people who are not poor while discouraging the poor from improving their communities. Since their rent is fixed as a proportion of their income, tenants cannot be penalized if maintenance and other operating costs rise, nor can many residents expect to gain from a reduction in these costs. In short, there is every reason for costs to rise and for nobody to care.

Privatizing Public Housing in Britain

There is evidence from experiments in the United States and abroad, however, that the economic and social dynamics of low-income housing can be altered, leading to improved conditions and reduced costs. Those experiments seem to have one thing in common—resident control. When low-income people acquire a financial stake in their own community, either by ownership or by direct control of the management function, their attitude toward housing changes dramatically. This can lead to actual reductions in the operating costs of buildings, as residents begin to recognize the importance of economizing. And it can also translate into dramatic reductions in the cost of social programs in the neighborhood as the general condition of the community becomes more important to those who live in it.

Proponents of the privatization approach recognize that public housing is not a collective good, since units are not jointly consumed. Costs can, in principle, be assigned to the residents and few would contend that public housing has positive externalities that warrant costs to be spread widely.

Given that public housing is more private than collective in nature, a possible solution to its problems would be to buy out the group that is the immediate cause of high costs by transferring ownership to the tenants, even at a loss. Government would lose part of the book value of its asset, of course, but there are reasons to suppose that privatization could significantly reduce both operating costs and negative externalities. Moreover, giving an ownership interest to the residents in this way could turn them into powerful allies against other interest groups that might lose by the transfer and its attendant cost savings.

As noted in Chapter 2, Britain has been highly successful in using the privatization approach to end expensive subsidies to thousands of units of public housing. When Margaret Thatcher took office, more than one-third of all British families lived in subsidized public housing. That proportion had grown steadily since World War I, chiefly because a coalition of beneficiaries—including housing suppliers and politicians—gained considerably from the expansion of the public sector. Tenants gained from subsidized rents, builders from the public-sector demand for construction, and socialist politicians from the strong constituency that developed around public housing. The socialist Labour party's policy that public housing should be of good quality and in desirable locations ensured that there would always be long waiting lists of near-beneficiaries, who formed a strong constituency pressing for more construction.

Conservatives seeking to control the growth and cost of public housing generally took the view that the appropriate policy was to reduce the subsidy by raising rents in line with tenants' incomes, thereby discouraging the nonpoor from demanding publicly owned units. Needless to say, Conservatives campaigning in public housing projects discovered that they could win few votes on a platform of raising rents. Public housing was so popular that residents who might have supported the Conservative party on most issues voted solidly for the Labour ticket in the hope of keeping their low-cost housing. Indeed, such a large number of relatively affluent working-class and lower-middle-class families live in British public housing that the mean family income is not far below that for owner-occupied housing.

Beginning in the early 1970s, Conservatives adopted a different strategy to reduce spending on public housing. Recognizing the home-ownership desires of the typical Briton, the Conservative government of Edward Heath permitted local housing authorities to sell units to sitting tenants at discounts of up to 50% of market price. Suddenly the politics of public housing changed. Instead of demanding that their rents be kept low, many residents began to demand ownership. Labour-controlled housing authorities generally tried to block sales, fearing the loss of a key constituency, but in most instances this merely antagonized would-be buyers. But the Thatcher government, elected in 1979, removed even this potential barrier by enacting a right-to-buy program, giving tenants the right to purchase their units at a discount of up to 50%—depending on how long they had resided in public housing—whether or not the local authority agreed.[3]

By instituting a discount purchase program, the Conservatives outbid the Labour party and bought out a key element of the public housing coalition. The effect of the program has been dramatic by any standard. During the period 1979–84, more than 500,000 units (out of a total stock of 7 million) have been sold, and sales are still strong. And where sales have taken place, neighborhood improvement undertaken by residents is evident. Moreover, the policy has paid off handsomely for the Conservatives in political terms. Buyers and would-be buyers have switched in droves to the Conservative banner. Thatcher's landslide 1983 general-election victory, several observers noted, was due in part to significant vote-switching among traditionally Labourite public housing tenants. *The New York Times* noted after the election that "As political experts and party strategists sift through the results of Labour's crushing defeat, . . . more and more are identifying the 'homeowner mentality' of voters . . . as a crucial development."[4]

Privatizing Public Housing in America

There are many differences between public housing in Britain and America. While more than 30% of the British population lives in public housing, for instance, the figure in America is below 1.5%. And while family incomes in British public housing span a wide range, public housing projects in America are generally populated by very low-income tenants, many of whom are on welfare. Projects in American cities have also been marked by broken families, drug use, and blight—problems that often affect neighboring communities. For this reason, many policymakers assume that public housing tenants are virtually beyond hope, and that notions of home ownership or resident management are simply fanciful.

American public housing, like any other federal program, also has a constituency that opposes significant change. Most tenants understandably prefer subsidized rents to market rents, and most seem to believe that the only real problem with public housing is that not enough money is spent on it. Housing developers and service contractors tend to agree.

Strong evidence shows, however, that the political dynamics of public housing can be changed, with significant benefits to residents, taxpayers, and neighboring communities. By transferring management responsibilities, and ultimately ownership, to associations of residents, it appears that enormous cost savings could be achieved. As housing authorities have begun to experiment with tenant management, the stereotypes of public housing tenants have been shattered. It has become increasingly clear that low-income people react to incentives and the opportunity to control their communities just as positively as anyone else.

Tenant management exists in many forms. In some instances it is token community control, with residents having little opportunity to shape their neighborhoods. In these situations, as one might expect, significant benefits have been hard to detect. But when real decision-making power is put into the hands of residents, and they are encouraged to innovate, the results can be startling. As head of Newark's public housing in the 1970s, for instance, Tom Massaro tried to tackle runaway costs in problem projects by inviting the tenants to take over many maintenance and other responsibilities. He opened up the books to tenant associations and offered them a deal: For every dollar they could save the city, 50 cents would be put into a fund to finance neighborhood activities. The result was a dramatic cut in vandalism and plummeting maintenance and utility costs—both creating major savings for the city. Similarly, the tenant association in a St. Louis project reversed deterioration and despair by recruiting residents to tackle social problems and improve maintenance. As one observer noted, the association "has transformed a neighborhood overrun with drug pushers and rats, with garbage heaps and abandoned units, into a model community. Today [the] public housing complex, Cochran Gardens, is so pleasant to live in that urban planners come from all over the United States, Great Britain, and Israel to copy it."[5]

One of the most successful and carefully studied tenant management associations is in Washington, D.C. The 464 Kenilworth-Parkside project was turned over to tenant management in 1982. By the end of 1983, according to a study by the American Enterprise Institute's Neighborhood Revitalization Project, administrative costs had been slashed by 63% compared with costs in 1981, and maintenance, the largest outlay, had dropped by 26%.[6] Rental income, moreover, increased by 60% over the same period, thanks to a reduced vacancy level and improved rent collection. Instead of being a considerable drain on the taxpayers, the project now runs at a healthy operating surplus.

The significant feature of the improvement in rental collection is that it came mainly from an increase in the income of tenants. This did not occur because welfare families were evicted and replaced with earning families, but because the association generated jobs for its members. It has established a thrift store, two day-care centers, a catering and cleaning business, a sandwich shop, its own co-op convenience store, and a barber shop and beauty parlor—all staffed by residents. In addition, residents developed the skills to undertake plumbing, electrical work, construction, and other maintenance tasks. Members of about one-third of the households in the project have obtained jobs associated with these ventures and management tasks.

By creating jobs within the project, the Kenilworth-Parkside association has increased family income while reducing housing costs. In so doing, it has cut the proportion of families on welfare from 85% to about 50% (or to 33% if young people in training are excluded). And as tenants have moved off welfare, the incentive for males to accept their family obligations has increased; families headed by women have fallen significantly, thanks to a 15% increase in the number of men moving back into the home, and the fact that the incidence of teenage pregnancy has been halved. This means not only that the taxpayer cost of operating subsidies has been cut, but also that federal and state outlays have been reduced for a host of welfare programs.

Such examples suggest that tenant management holds great potential as a method both of reducing public housing and of cutting welfare costs. Privatization of the management function in this way should thus be considered a general approach to dealing with the costs and problems of public housing. However, obstacles to privatization should not be underestimated, even though they are solvable.

In the first place, management skills are not acquired overnight. They have to be learned—and they are best learned from other tenant managers. This takes time. But the process is accelerating, thanks to the efforts of the Washington-based National Center for Neighborhood Enterprise. This private organization has established a network of tenant management groups, enabling technical information to be exchanged and novice managers to avoid the mistakes committed by their predecessors.

A second barrier is resistance from those who feel threatened by tenant management. That can include some residents. If a tenant association is to be successful, it has to root out community troublemakers such as pimps and drug pushers. But these troublemakers rarely go quietly, and several associations report that they have had to defend lawsuits charging discrimination or infringement of civil rights—brought against them by career criminals. On occasion, some tenant managers complain, these suits are even pursued with the assistance of attorneys supplied by the ACLU or the Legal Services Corporation.

Managers and contractors of the nation's Public Housing Authorities may also feel threatened by tenant associations. Tenant responsibility for management and maintenance means fewer sinecures and sugar-coated contracts for friends of PHA officials. Consequently, it is often the PHA owners of projects who do most to discourage tenant management and try to render it ineffective once it has been instituted.

If the privatization of public housing management is to be encouraged, it would therefore be most unwise to rely on the PHAs to initiate or sustain the process. The greatest benefits would be achieved where the PHA is corrupt or grossly inefficient, but such an authority is hardly likely to promote a more honest or efficient alternative. To break the impasse the best course might be for the U.S. Department of Housing and Urban Development (HUD) to seek legislation or rule changes to require PHAs to experiment with HUD-designed tenant management programs as a condition for receiving operating subsidies or modernization funds. In this way, conservative budget cutters at the federal level might forge a privatization coalition with public housing residents seeking to improve their community. Together the two groups could isolate PHA officials and others who favor the current program structure.

Privatizing public housing management, of course, falls far short of complete privatization. That would mean transferring ownership to the tenants, as in Britain. Complete privatization would have important advantages compared with the privatization of management. It would, for instance, allow residents to enjoy an asset appreciation from improvements in the community, giving them a stronger incentive to work for neighborhood stability. It would allow low income people to move up to the first rung of the ladder of financial benefits associated with ownership. And it would protect residents from possible displacement and other uncertainties associated with government ownership of their homes.

Most analysts and HUD officials have assumed that any true ownership program necessarily would have to be confined to a tiny fraction of tenants, because few tenants have management and maintenance skills or sufficient income to cover even operating costs, let alone finance charges. But such calculations ignore the results of tenant management.

A British-style ownership program, with tenant management as the intermediate stage, could be an effective method of turning public housing tenants into homeowners. The administration is working with favorable PHAs, under existing law, to enable successful tenant management associations to become cooperatives and then allow these cooperatives to purchase their projects at a discount. Once several successful demonstration projects had been undertaken and publicized, the administration should be able to count on wider political support, especially from near-beneficiary tenant groups, for a more extensive program. The logical next step would be to request from Congress a right-to-buy law modeled on the popular British program. The law should allow tenant groups to apply for ownership directly to the Secretary of HUD. For those who are eligible, HUD would set in motion the ownership process, with or without the local PHA's approval.

Under this right-to-buy proposal, a tenant management association, after appropriate training, would take over maintenance and other operations of the project—including garbage collection and routine curb maintenance contracts. Whatever the association achieved in cost reductions would be placed in an escrow account toward the purchase price. Previous savings achieved by existing associations would be credited to their account.

When the cash available in the account and the lower operating costs accomplished by the association reached levels that made ownership feasible, the association would be allowed to buy part or all of the project on a co-op basis at 30% of the market value when the application was first made. No down payment would be required. If a member of the resident co-op sold his or her share within the first year, the entire 70% discount would be repayable. This repayable portion would fall to zero over seven years. A discount repayable on a sliding scale would have a similar equity effect on a conventional down payment, encouraging buyers to stay in the property and maintain it even though they would have no cash tied up in it. Under this proposal, the association could obtain the mortgage from whatever source it wished, but it would have the right to a mortgage from the PHA (much like a private owner taking back a mortgage), so financing would be ensured.

The political future for both partial and complete privatization of public housing looks bright. The strategy enables fiscal conservatives to reduce outlays by offering to empower low-income urban residents: an unusual coalition but, as Britain has shown, a powerful one. Typical of the privatization approach, both the management and ownership plans would detach key elements of a public spending coalition and turn them into a private-sector coalition. By starting in a small way with a demonstration project, existing law could be used to achieve a visible success as a focus for building up political support to expand the program among other public housing tenants and former skeptics. As management functions and properties were transferred, the need for operating subsidies would diminish. And if the experience so far is any indication, welfare costs would also fall.

As the right-to-buy program demonstrated in Britain, the urge to own a home is a powerful force. The prospect of ownership and the control over one's life that goes with it can effect a major change in behavior patterns. The British discovered that tenants who had long enjoyed heavily subsidized rents were prepared to forgo them once they were allowed to own. In America, the experience of tenant management suggests that the same is true of even very low-income people and that they will reduce costs dramatically if they have an incentive to do so. The privatization of public housing management and ownership, in other words, offers the chance to relieve the pressure on operating subsidies and social costs in public projects by shifting demand entirely out of the public sector, to the benefit of taxpayer and resident alike.

Amtrak

The National Railroad Passenger Corporation, or Amtrak, was created under the 1970 Rail Passenger Service Act in an effort to reverse the decline in the nation's intercity rail passenger service by relieving rail freight companies of the burden of providing passenger services. The act did this by empowering the federal government to operate such services.

Although Amtrak, like public housing, provides a private good to private citizens, it is perceived by the public as a different kind of federal asset. Public housing evokes little pride among typical taxpayers. But merely the mention of trains on a radio call-in show is guaranteed to jam the switchboard with calls from listeners prepared to reminisce about their childhood adventures on the Empire Builder or the San Francisco Zephyr. Americans like trains—even those who would never dream of riding on one for a normal business trip.

Paradoxically, the average citizen's soft spot for passenger trains has made federal ownership of the passenger system a poor method of serving their purposes. In theory, federal ownership should have meant that Amtrak would in some sense serve the national interest. Instead, it has resulted in the typical dynamics of federal programs: Amtrak provides enormous benefits to a small constituency, at a cost of close to $1 billion a year in operating subsidies alone. Only by changing these dynamics can we eliminate this constant drain on the Treasury.

The Dynamics of Amtrak

In 1920 there were twenty thousand passenger trains in America. By 1967 there were five hundred. The principal reason for this decline was the growth of competing modes of transport, particularly automobiles and commercial aircraft. By the 1960s, railroads were actively discouraging passengers so that they could obtain permission from the Interstate Commerce Commission to abandon routes by demonstrating a lack of public demand.

By the late 1960s, it was clear that many private railroads would have to discontinue passenger routes or face bankruptcy. Rather than allowing them to shed the services, letting passenger services go the way of the stagecoach, Congress moved, under lobbying pressure from the National Association of Rail Passengers, to create a new corporation to provide passenger services with federal subsidies. Amtrak is a hybrid corporation. All but four members of its 13-member board are presidential appointees, yet it also has private shareholders in the form of railroads that joined the system in 1971, thereby obtaining the right to discontinue passenger services under their own auspices. Amtrak owns its own equipment and employs service attendants. Except in the Northeast Corridor, however, Amtrak owns no rights-of-way. It must contract with private railroads for trackage rights and train crews.

Under the "rescue" plan, Amtrak received $40 million in operating grants in 1971 and a further $100 million in capital loans. Congress intended this to be a one-time aid package to turn the numerous unprofitable passenger rail services into one profitable system. But as a 1982 Congressional Budget Office (CBO) study reported, "Despite original Congressional intent to form a self-supporting corporation, Amtrak has never covered its costs with passenger revenues and has become increasingly dependent on federal assistance."[7]

Operating grants have risen steadily, reaching $719 million in 1981. Loans increased to $400 million a year by 1975. After that date the federal government ceased to provide capital loans; it recognized the inevitable and gave grants instead. By 1981, annual federal assistance was over $1 billion a year, and total federal assistance was close to $8 billion. In that year, "federal subsidies made up about 60% of Amtrak's operating costs (less depreciation) with subsidies averaging about $37 per passenger."[8] Congress apparently accepted the reality of the financial mess in 1978: It changed Amtrak's description from "for profit" to "managed and operated as a for profit corporation."

Annual report after annual report issued by Amtrak still speaks glowingly of the progress made in cost reduction and efficiency. But, says the CBO, much of the apparent improvement on specific routes "seems to stem from adjustments in Amtrak's allocation method, not from real declines in financial losses or increases in ridership." The congressional analysts are extremely pessimistic about the corporation's ability to improve its performance with its present structure of services:

> Although there is some potential for reducing Amtrak's future dependence on federal subsidies by cutting costs or increasing revenues from existing services, that potential is likely to be marginal and holds little prospect for substantially reducing Amtrak's subsidy needs. The need for subsidies can be reduced substantially only by trimming services.[9]

The obvious question for the taxpayer to ask is "Why not then cut services?" There are certainly plenty of trains that run with few passengers and many losses. The answer is that a highly effective public spending coalition ensures that Congress will do little to reduce costly services. As Jeffrey Shedd explains, this coalition got off to an early start with the creation of the system in 1970:

> Amtrak's route structure was to be designated by the Secretary of transportation, in consultation with Congress, the ICC, rail labor organizations, the National Association of Railroad Passengers (NARP), and others. As the route designation process ground slowly on, with each group wanting more and more trains added to the minimal system originally proposed by Transportation Secretary Volpe, it became clear that one of Amtrak's major problems would be to operate a successful railroad over a politicized route structure.[10]

The coalition has the best of all possible worlds. It has the political power to entrench its interests against those who attack long-distance passenger services as structurally uneconomic. And it can send the tab for the uneconomic service to the taxpayers, who seem willing to accept it, apparently believing that trains are an integral part of the American way.

Amtrak passengers should be very grateful for the taxpayers' assistance, because it is exceedingly generous. The taxpayers subsidized every passenger who took a ride on the Amtrak system in 1981, to the tune of nearly $38 on average—up from $32 in 1980. On long-distance routes the subsidy was closer to $100, up from $78 in 1980. Even on the well-traveled Northeast Corridor route, the subsidy amounted to more than $18 per traveler. Throughout the whole Amtrak system, passenger revenues *and* local subsidies covered less than 40% percent of costs in 1981—Uncle Sam picked up the remainder.[11]

The CBO calculates that Amtrak's cost per real mile is three times greater than that for bus travel and 50% greater than for travel by air. And while each mode of transportation does receive subsidies in various forms, the 1980 federal subsidy per passenger mile on Amtrak was 23.6¢, compared with 0.2¢ for commercial aviation, and 0.1¢ each for buses and private automobiles.[12] The government would save money on many Amtrak routes if it simply provided existing passengers with free airline tickets and shut the railroad routes down. As Arizona transportation expert John Semmens pointed out in a 1982 study:

> On a trip from Phoenix, Arizona, to Los Angeles, California, for instance, the Amtrak fare is about $60. Amtrak's cost of providing service is approximately $280. The taxpayer bill for each person carried is $220, or nearly 80% of the cost. In contrast, a flight between the same two points costs the passenger about $40 in fare and user taxes.[13]

Some proponents of Amtrak respond to such figures by arguing that subsidies are justified, in order to provide inexpensive transportation for low-income Americans. Yet the data show that Amtrak serves middle- and upper-income people, not the poor. Figures available to the CBO revealed that, in 1977, persons with income below $5,000 took 17% of all trips by bus, compared with 7% of trips by train. In contrast, 53% of train trips were taken by persons with incomes of more than $20,000—an income group that accounted for just 28% of bus trips.[14] Amtrak, in other words, is a billion-dollar-a-year program to transport middle-class Americans who like trains—and who vote.

Passengers are only one element of the coalition, however. High labor costs are a significant contributor to Amtrak's poor economic condition. The corporation's annual per worker costs are greater than those in the bus industry and compare well with those in the airline industry. Yet measured in passenger and seat miles per labor year, bus and air productivity is about triple that of Amtrak. A major reason for this is that when Amtrak was created, Congress agreed to union demands that the corporation should use the work rules of its contracting railroads. So the inefficiency that contributed to the demise of private passenger railroads was built into the new corporation.

An example of these arrangements is the 100-mile rule, under which crews are paid a full day's pay for each hundred-mile trip. This can lead to very generous payments to train crews. A 1978 study by the General Accounting Office, for instance, found that the pair of two-man crews on the five-hour, 40-minute run from Detroit to Chicago received an average of 1.4 days' pay per crew member.[15] And on the Montrealer run from Washington to New York, Shedd notes, the Conrail crew members receive two days' pay for their 270 minutes of work.[16] Needless to say, train crews are quite happy with federal support for Amtrak.

Politicians are very sensitive to the benefits received by passengers and employees of the system, and they hear little anger from the 99% of taxpayers who do not use Amtrak for intercity travel. Consequently, the politicians are not inclined to change things and risk the ire of the Amtrak coalition. Predictably, the routes that are safest from the congressional ax tend to be those that meander through the greatest number of congressional districts. The money-losing Montrealer, Shedd calculates, services at least forty-six House districts and passes through nine states as it travels from Washington to Montreal—more than enough to attract solid political support in Congress.

The Amtrak coalition has been remarkably effective in neutralizing threats to its federal support. When President Ford sought to make cutbacks in 1975, for instance, Amtrak responded by testifying that the only way it could meet the president's targets was by eliminating services that just happened to run through the districts of key congressmen. Not surprisingly, Congress showed little interest in Ford's plan. Similarly, President Carter's attempt to reduce route mileage by 43% was stymied by effective lobbying, and by gas shortages which temporarily boosted ridership.[17] President Reagan's efforts have fared little better.

It is interesting to compare the chronic loss-making of Amtrak with the solid turnaround of Conrail, the freight rail system created in 1976 out of the shambles of six failing northeastern railroads. Conrail has also swallowed large amounts of taxpayer money—some $7 billion in all—but the nationalized railroad has not needed any federal money in four years. It now makes a handsome profit, and the Reagan administration announced in the summer of 1984 that it was ready to sell the railroad back to the private sector.

Fortunately for the American taxpayer, the politics and economics of Conrail have been different from those of Amtrak, allowing the railroad to develop a rational structure and to be privatized in an orderly way. There are good reasons for this. In the first place, the rail freight industry may have been in the doldrums, but it is not yet obsolete—unlike rail passenger services. So employees and users had the incentive to work toward independence from government and the long-run stability that goes with profitability. In addition, and perhaps even more important, Conrail is a regional system that has been unable to enjoy the political support that comes with a national system or the public's love affair with passenger trains. Consequently, the coalition gaining from the Conrail subsidies was never able to achieve the status of permanent dependent of the federal government. That position is reserved for Amtrak.

Privatizing Amtrak

It is conceivable that if Amtrak deficits continue to grow rapidly (and there is every reason to believe that they will), Congress and the American taxpayer will one day tire of the staggering cost and demand radical financial surgery. But that day may be a long time in coming. Amtrak was supposed to require only a one-shot injection of $140 million to put it in good shape. Thirteen years and $11 billion later it is in worsening financial health, and yet the taxpayers still seem willing to pick up the tab.

Amtrak is likely to continue running up enormous deficits as long as its beneficiaries have no incentive to economize. Privatization, however, could achieve that change of incentives within the current political climate by altering the ownership structure. Placing ownership in the hands of private-sector organizations would bring efficiency pressures to the railroad while reducing or eliminating taxpayer funding of the system. Winning support for such privatization would not be an easy task, however. Existing beneficiaries have no incentives, at least on the face of it, to give up federal aid in return for ownership responsibilities. And other constituencies would seem to have little reason to buy stock in a private Amtrak, given its precarious situation and low ridership.

The first step toward successful privatization is to recognize that the system is really three systems: the Northeast Corridor, which accounts for more than half the trains and passengers carried; short-distance routes outside the Northeast; and long-distance routes. The losses are heavily concentrated in the long-distance routes. Indeed, if only short-term avoidable costs are considered (costs for crews, fuel, and supplies), the CBO estimates that the 1981 loss on the Northeast Corridor route was just $6 million, compared with $36 million on the short-distance routes and $139 million on the long-distance routes.[18]

Given that no segments of the Amtrak system show even an operating surplus (and thus a contribution to fixed costs), it would be in the interests of the taxpayers for the government to *give away* the system to anyone willing to take it. Few people, of course, would want a loss-making route, but the employees of Amtrak might be interested in a gift of the Northeast Corridor route, which is the closest to breaking even on operating costs. If the employees were given title to that heavily used route, free of all debt, they would have the incentive to change their own work rules to improve the efficiency of operations on the route and thereby increase the value of their stock. As the privatization of Britain's National Freight Corporation demonstrated, inefficient employees of loss-making nationalized firms can become remarkably productive once they become owners.

Such a move would recognize the futility of trying to defeat an entrenched and powerful coalition by seeking congressional support for closing down lines and denying service to passengers. Instead it would provide an incentive for a key segment of the Amtrak coalition to find methods of decreasing costs. Moreover, by dividing up Amtrak in this way, and detaching a portion of the constituency, political resistance to cuts in other parts of the system would be weakened.

The seemingly hopeless financial condition of the long-distance Amtrak routes makes even a giveaway to employees impossible; no rational person would accept the gift of an enterprise that loses $100 on every customer. For these segments of Amtrak, every effort needs to be made to encourage passengers to choose other means of transport, thereby relieving Amtrak of the demand for its services. Increasing fares would have this effect, although both passengers and staff would oppose that policy.

Increases in fares might be made politically palatable, however, if wider publicity were given to the subsidies per passenger and the income characteristics of those passengers. Differential pricing, which is common in railroads in Europe, might also be used to reduce resistance to fare increases. In Britain, for instance, categories of rail passengers deemed to be in special financial need, such as students and senior citizens, are provided with passes that give them the right to substantial discounts on rail fares. If senior citizens, welfare recipients, and other groups were provided with passes entitling them to fare discounts on Amtrak, it would be easier for the administration to press Congress to raise fares for the non-needy in order to discourage ridership.

Amtrak represents one of the most difficult types of programs to cut, even when utilizing the privatization technique. It gives heavy benefits to middle-class passengers, who tend to be politically active. Because Amtrak provides a subsidy in service and not in cash, moreover, both passengers and taxpayers typically have no appreciation of the subsidy involved. The physical presence of Amtrak in so many states and congressional districts also adds a political interest far in excess of the direct beneficiaries involved. And the nostalgia felt for train services increases taxpayer inertia, making budget constraints difficult to sustain.

The partial privatization model suggested above takes account of the distorted economics of Amtrak and its peculiar politics. The carrot of employee ownerhip has proved a very effective device in Britain for dividing up public spending coalitions and turning loss making firms into profitable ones. Using this approach on the Northeast Corridor could save the one part of Amtrak that appears viable, while detaching East Coast businessmen, and their congressional representatives, from their alliance with train lovers in the West. If this breech could be accomplished, congressional support for increased user charges to discourage demand might be obtainable. In the long run, such an approach could stem the flood of subsidies and allow the federal government to extricate itself at last from the business of transporting Americans at heavy taxpayer cost.

Public Lands

Public housing and Amtrak both represent publicly held assets that provide private benefits to individuals. Few proponents of these programs maintain that the assets are true collective or common-pool goods. They argue instead that public ownership is necessary to ensure a stream of benefits to a group of supposedly worthy recipients.

Public lands represent another type of federal asset, and the arguments supporting government ownership are very different. Public lands, it is said, are collective goods in that they provide benefits to all Americans—benefits that would not be ensured if the lands were in private ownership. Yet, as we shall see, these assumptions are seriously flawed. Many individuals and corporations obtain private and commercial benefits from certain public lands courtesy of the taxpayers. And even for the more genuinely public tracts, private ownership would lead to more effective utilization for the public interest.

Implications of Federal Ownership

There are approximately 2.25 billion acres of land within the United States. Of this, 742 million acres, or about 33% of the total, is owned by federal, state, and local governments. In the West, the federal government owns about 50% of all land, including 89% of Alaska, 86% of Nevada, and 46% of California. About 92% of all public lands are concentrated in twelve western states.[19]

Federal holdings of land may be broken down into three broad categories, each with distinctive characteristics: grazing land, where ranchers have surface-use rights; timberland, where trees can be harvested privately; and wilderness or wildlife preserves. In addition, the federal government owns various tiny parcels of land, some of it in metropolitan areas. There are also mineral resources on certain tracts, which are leased to private concerns.

Although it might be comforting to think that such lands are held and utilized "in the public interest," there are two very good reasons why they are not. The first is that although federal administrators are, in a sense, managers acting on behalf of all citizens, they are subject to few of the normal pressures that would apply to private-sector managers. They have little incentive, in short, to maximize benefits for the owners.

Until the turn of this century, federal land policy had two fairly clear goals: facilitating settlement and raising revenue. Both these objectives stimulated the transfer of land to private individuals. The transfer was not carried out in an ideal way—burdensome rules and the rigid homestead grid caused many problems—but at least the advantages of private ownership began to be felt. The problems started when federal agencies began to manage lands rather than disposing of them. Surveying the literature on federal ownership, Interior Department economist Robert Nelson notes that

> Economic researchers have found that efficient use of resources is seldom a main criterion in decisions made by public land managers. As a result, public land management exhibits pervasive inefficiencies, including allocation of public land to lower over higher value uses, investments for which costs substantially exceed the benefits, investments

made in one place where other places would offer much higher returns, the conservation of public resources where their immediate production would be appropriate, or, conversely, the current production of public resources where reserving them for future use instead would be appropriate.[20]

Despite managing assets worth hundreds of billions of dollars, observes Nelson, the federal government continues to operate them at a loss. Bureaucratically assigned use rights encourage inefficient utilization of range land, and the Forest Service succeeds in losing money even though "most timber currently harvested comes from 'old growth' forests on which little money has been invested."[21] Were federal land policy to eschew any hint of commercial objectives in order to reach environmental preservation goals, the approach might be justified—if lopsided. But it does not. In fact, many practices are both inefficient and environmentally damaging. Analysts John Baden and Richard Stroup argue that, in fact, the greatest danger to the environment may lie in the federal subsidy of otherwise uneconomic activities.[22] As the Bureau of Land Management has exercised greater control over grazing rights, for instance, it has discouraged ranchers from making investments that would tend to preserve the range.

The second reason why public ownership of land does not mean it is managed according to any consensus of "the public interest" is that when ownership responsibility is divorced from group interests, there is no mechanism to bring about an orderly balance of these interests. Consequently, each special interest has an incentive to demand that the land be utilized according to its own goals, without regard to the costs that imposes on competing groups. Hunters and recreationists, for instance, have the incentive to demand access and family facilities, just as preservationists have the incentive to oppose excessive hunting, hotels, and roads, and mining companies the incentive to demand commercial access.

Each group can further its interests only through the political process when land is held by the federal government. Instead of exchanging property rights and balancing the costs and benefits of alternative uses, as private owners would do, these interest groups lobby the government, and they are not satisfied unless they dominate the process. Interior Secretary James Watt ran afoul of the environmentalists by ignoring the reality of their political strength. But in many ways his dilemma was inescapable; like any manager of public lands, he was asked to perform the impossible task of satisfying competing interests that had no incentive to compromise.

The Importance of Private Ownership

Public lands are not "public," or collective, in the economic meaning of the word. They are not lands, in other words, that can be used only jointly by all citizens, conveying no benefits that could be charged for on an individual basis. Far from it. Most public rangeland provides distinct benefits to individual ranchers, thanks to their grazing rights. Timber and minerals companies obtain tangible commercial benefits from their lease rights. And hunters and vacationers derive distinct individual enjoyment from the land. In each instance individuals could be excluded and fees levied.

Even in those situations where a resource is in some sense available to all, it does not follow that federal ownership guarantees that the land will be utilized in the common interest. Privately owned herds of cattle are carefully protected by their owners, while buffalo and whales have been slaughtered without regard to the long-term consequences. And trees and wildlife are plentiful in Maine, despite—indeed, because of—almost universal private ownership and management. As Baden and Stroup explain:

> There are examples of situations handled politically in this country—with dubious results—that are handled through a system of private ownership in other parts of the world—with admirable results. Scotland has no government agency to protect water quality. Yet its streams run as pure and clean as any of us would have American streams. How does it happen? Individual Scots have clearly defined and transferable (salable) rights to the streams, so incidents of pollution or diversion constitute damage to individuals, not failure to meet government standards, and are treated as such in the courts.[23]

When the government owns a resource, decisions pertaining to its use are necessarily political in nature. Rather than reflecting the interests of "the people" as owners, they are the result of political pressure; whoever can wield the greatest lobbying power will exercise the greatest control over the asset. When individuals or groups have clear property rights over land, on the other hand, they have a strong incentive both to maintain it and to maximize its long-run returns.

The task confronting the privatizer is to find a method of ascribing property rights over land in such a way that the general public does not subsidize private interests, that an orderly balance is struck between competing interests, and that private property rights are assigned within wilderness and other sensitive lands in such a way that they are preserved and open to the public. And the privatizer must do this in a way that takes account of the political power of existing proprietary interests.

The Reagan administration has already experienced the pitfalls associated with even modest privatization when that policy does not take full account of existing *de facto* private property rights over "public" land. Early in 1982, President Reagan approved a proposal to allow the government to "dispose of unneeded public lands." The program was to be very modest: Interior Secretary James Watt announced that no more than 5% of public lands, or about 35 million acres, would be sold, and an initial audit by the Bureau of Land Management identified only 4.4 million acres as prime prospects for sale—less than 3% of the government's holdings in the contiguous forty-eight states. Nevertheless, wrote Bruce Ramsey, the suggestion to sell off even this small amount of federal land proved to be "about as popular as a personal attack on Smokey the Bear."[24]

The press portrayed the program as a transfer of enormous proportions. *Time* magazine, for instance, called the proposal the "land sale of the century," and columnist Jack Anderson cautioned that if the sale were not handled with the utmost care, it could turn into "one of the biggest land grabs by private interests in the nation's history."[25] Of course, these critics overlooked the fact that an average of nearly 100,000 acres of public land was sold each year during the 1950s and 1960s. Not surprisingly, self-appointed custodians of the public interest lost little time in denouncing the proposed sale. The Sierra Club attacked the program as a "Master Plan for Government Giveaways."[26] And according to Gordon Roberts of the Wilderness Society, the administration was "promoting the outright piracy of lands that belong to the American people."[27]

The privatization strategy outlined in Chapter 2 emphasizes the critical importance of creating a privatization coalition that benefits from the transfer to the private sector, to counter the established interests favoring retention in the federal domain. Yet the administration's proposal received a lukewarm reaction from the very private-sector interests that one might assume would have been its strongest proponents. The main reason for this was that formal privatization posed a potential threat to informal private-property rights already established under federal ownership. Ranchers, for instance, acquired grazing rights on segments of public lands under the 1934 Taylor Grazing Act. These rights were attached to particular parcels of private lands, adding to their value. In some instances the value of private tracts has been increased substantially by virtue of the attached grazing rights.

Consequently, talk of selling land by competitive bid constituted a direct threat to ranchers, since the low-priced grazing rights were capitalized into their ranch values. Despite attempts by the administration to find some way of accommodating existing rights, many ranchers felt they had little to gain and much to lose from the privatization effort. Even though the program was modest in scale, writes Nelson, many ranchers believed that the sales "might have provided a precedent which would occur in the future. Rather than open the way for such a possibility, ranchers and other traditional western land users joined with environmentalists and other national interest groups to seek to eliminate the entire privatization effort."[28]

The administration initiative also gained little support among timber industry lobbyists. According to a White House senior economist, Steve Hanke, who designed key elements of the administration plan, even a very limited sale of the national forest timberland would have raised well over $100 billion while providing the industry with valuable timber-growing land. Opposition from environmentalists and outdoor groups was bitter but predictable, and no constituency emerged to back the proposal. According to timber industry specialist Luke Popovich, writing at the time in *American Forests* magazine, privatization was "unsettling to the cozy fraternity of public officials and industry and environmental lobbyists" in Washington. "Industry lobbyists were uninterested in privatizing what they enjoyed at cost."[29] Given the choice between paying a market price to own timberland and paying the government to harvest trees that the taxpayer has maintained, timber companies prefer to lobby rather than to own. "Industry is generally not interested in free enterprise," says Barney Dowdle, forestry professor at the University of Washington. "They're interested in subsidized wood."[30]

Had Interior Secretary Watt been a supporter of privatization (which, according to Hanke and others, he was not), and had President Reagan tried to go over the heads of the industry lobbyists to explain to the people the rationale behind his move, the privatization initiative might have gained a political toehold. Instead, the administration backed off rapidly in the face of hostility, and the privatization effort was quietly abandoned.

Formalizing Informal Privatization

Although the Reagan administration's privatization initiative failed, it did occasion some rethinking by the experts about the potential of market forces for balancing environmental interests. As Popovich notes, "a growing number of academics, public officials, conservationists, and even a few thinking environmental-ists are looking beyond the draconian misconceptions of privatiza-tion."[31] Yet this increasing sympathy for the logic of private own-ership will never be turned into a successful policy unless its sup-porters can break up the public-ownership coalition and create a new coalition with a proprietary interest in privatization.

The key to such a strategy is to design it with careful regard to the informal privatization that currently exists. As mentioned ear-lier, ranchers have *de facto* property rights over rangeland by vir-tue of their grazing rights. Similarly, argues Nelson, wilderness organizations have demonstrated their ability to control the use of certain public lands, while not owning them, through their politi-cal successes in battles over drilling rights. As a result of their suc-cess, *de facto* privatization of wilderness has occurred, "although the private rights created in this case are collective rather than individual. Wilderness user groups have established a claim to control use of wilderness areas at least as strong as ranchers have asserted over use of grazing land allotments."[32] Of course a dis-tinction must be drawn between the rights obtained by ranchers and those acquired by wilderness groups. Ranchers have paid for their rights. The IRS recognizes them, and ranchers even pay pro-perty taxes on their permits. The wilderness groups enjoy rights resulting only from political muscle; they might best be described as "political property rights."

Yet this informal privatization has serious drawbacks, both for the "owners" of the informal rights and for the orderly manage-ment of the land. The uncertainty surrounding their rights, for instance, discourages many ranchers from investing in rangeland improvements. Even more important from an orderly manage-ment perspective, informal rights cannot be bought and sold, so conflicting objectives cannot be resolved by trading rights. "If wilderness groups actually owned wilderness areas," explains Nel-son, "they might be willing to sell some oil and gas drilling rights, where the large resulting revenues could be used to purchase further wilderness areas. Under the existing system, they can defend their use rights and successfully exclude oil and gas drilling from wilderness areas, but cannot waive these rights for a direct cash payment."[33]

In fact, some wilderness groups *do* own wilderness lands, and they do trade rights. The National Audubon Society owns seventy-five wildlife sanctuaries totaling over 200,000 acres, the largest of which is the 26,000-acre Rainey Wildlife Sanctuary in Louisiana. The refuge is so sensitive that tourists are unwelcome, and yet three oil companies operate gas wells in the sanctuary, providing the Audubon Society with $300,000 a year in royalties.[34]

The Audubon Society has a cooperative working relationship with the oil companies. The environmentalists require the companies to use methods that meet the society's objectives, while the royalties enable the society to purchase and maintain more wilderness areas. Its ownership of the sanctuary, in other words, encourages the society to allow the extraction of minerals in a carefully managed way, so that it can finance other purchases and activities. Were the Rainey Sanctuary federally owned, the Audubon Society would have every incentive to oppose any commercial activity, since the society would gain nothing from commercial operations.

Baden and Stroup argue that the lesson to be learned from such examples is that wilderness lands should be *given* to qualified environmental groups such as the Audubon Society, the Sierra Club, and the Wilderness Society. As Baden points out: "With fee simple title to the land, the wilderness group is forced by its own criteria to consider the opportunity cost of nondevelopment.... [All] interested parties would become more constructive in their thinking and their language."[35] This would lead environmentalists, say Baden and Stroup, to balance the desire to block all commercial activity with the incentive to use revenues to acquire more wilderness land.

The Baden-Stroup proposal could be decisive in altering the political dynamics of public lands. It recognizes that environmental groups do have a powerful influence over wilderness land policy—and hence informal property rights—and turns these into legal rights so that they can be traded. In this way the environmentalists would have an incentive to act as rational and responsible owners on behalf of the American people. By removing the threat to environmentalists implicit in federal ownership, the plan would encourage them to give more favorable consideration to some commercial use of the land—especially as such uses would provide them with more revenue to buy and protect other areas. Moving slowly with such transfers (Baden and Stroup suggest 5% of wilderness lands in the first instance) would enable the environmentalists to acquire management capacity and begin to generate revenues from lease sales and royalties, so that further tracts could be released to them.

Giving popular environmental groups legal ownership of sensitive wilderness areas (and possibly timberland of significant interest to conservationists) would put to rest many of the public's fears concerning the use of "public" lands. It would also help to break up the unholy alliance of interest groups that currently oppose transferring lands to private ownership. Doing this would make it a little easier for would-be privatizers to isolate those ranchers and timber companies who gain great private benefits from public ownership. These interests could be isolated further by the publication of research data from inside and outside the administration, showing the implicit subsidy to private commercial interests associated with federal ownership.

If environmentalist opposition to privatization could be muted in this way, the administration could turn to the issue of grazing and timberland—this time with its political flank covered. The ranchers' criticism of the 1982 privatization plan might be softened by formally recognizing the informal (but paid for) property rights associated with grazing privileges. Steve Hanke suggests giving ranchers with permits the option of gaining title by buying the permit, on a first refusal basis, at a price equal to the discounted present value of the ranchers' projected annual grazing fees. "In effect," says Hanke, "ranchers would be charged for only that portion of the permit's value that had not already been paid for through premiums for private land."[36] If a rancher refused the option, the permit would be sold to the highest bidder, and the rancher would receive the difference between the bid and the option price. Buying out the existing proprietary interests of ranchers in this way would enable privatization to take place—giving the incentive to ranchers to invest in the once-public lands, without threatening existing informal rights.

Timberland poses fewer difficulties for the privatizer. An increase in charges to firms now enjoying subsidies, together with outright sale of nonsensitive forests to private companies (with the caveat that hunting and public access must not be denied) should be feasible once the wilderness and rangeland questions have been settled.

The recent resistance to private ownership of western lands seems strange, given the history of settlement in the United States, until one recognizes that informal ownership does exist and that the beneficiaries are doing very well in the existing arrangement. Privatization will fail if it ignores these informal rights. But if a strategy is designed that enshrines these rights, and buys out the environmentalist lobby, it may well be possible to establish formal private rights over these lands in a manner that raises revenue for the beleaguered taxpayer, allows rational priorities to be established for land use, and buffers wilderness management politics.

These examples of asset privatization illustrate the range of asset types held by the federal government, and the coalitions that gain from their retention in the federal domain. Other federal assets, such as the Washington airports, debt portfolios, and federal power plants, could be examined in the same way. They are subject to similar political forces and amenable to similar privatization solutions.

In each example, public ownership either denies the taxpayers income they should receive (from certain public lands) or costs them enormous sums because the prevailing incentives encourage inappropriate spending and inefficiency (Amtrak and public housing). Privatization's two themes—private ownership and the importance of coalitions—address these deficiencies and their associated budget costs in a way that traditional cost-cutting cannot. By altering the ownership structure of the asset, the strategy would cause people to make wiser economic decisions. And by using the ownership carrot to break up existing coalitions and build new ones, it would alter fundamentally the political balance. In this way, it would allow the federal government to extricate itself from the costly ownership of loss-making concerns that actually serve private interests.

4

HUMAN SERVICES

Other than Social Security, the most important component of the expansion of federal spending in recent years has been outlays on programs designed to assist low-income Americans. Spending on such "income-conditioned" programs amounted to less than $4 billion in 1960, before President Johnson's Great Society legislation was enacted. By 1970 the figure had reached $16.7 billion, or 1.68% of GNP, and by 1980 it had climbed to $73.3 billion, or 2.78%. As a proportion of the federal budget, such spending rose from 8.5% in 1970 to 12.7% in 1980.[1] Clearly it will be difficult to accomplish any major cutback in the size of the federal government until significant changes are made in this highly sensitive element of spending.

As discussed in Chapter 1, the growth of federal human-services programs reflects both a change in public attitudes and the remarkable political success of public spending coalitions. The New Deal and Great Society programs, in particular, were driven by the liberal belief in the notion of a national community: that the country as a whole, as distinct from individuals and local communities, has an obligation to assist the less fortunate. And once the basic programs were in place, sophisticated coalitions were able to build on them in an incremental fashion, assisted by the inherent political advantage the spender enjoys over the taxpayer.

Human-services programs can best be broken down into two, or perhaps three, distinct types. These categories reveal that very different issues are often involved in reforming each program in a way that would cut unnecessary spending while discharging society's obligations to those in need.

The first, and most important, set of services comprises those that concern goods and services that are truly private goods, as defined in Chapter 2. A market does operate for these needs, but the low-income person or family simply does not have the means to purchase an adequate supply. This category would include assistance programs for food and clothing, such as food stamps and Aid to Families with Dependent Children; for housing, Section 8 rent assistance, for example, and the new voucher program; for health care, chiefly Medicaid; and for training and education. In each instance the federal program either provides recipients with the means to purchase their requirements in the marketplace or, less commonly, operates a federal service alongside the private sector—in providing legal services for the poor, for example.

The second category of human services consists of those where a private market does not really exist or where individuals would be unlikely to avail themselves of the service even if they were given financial assistance. These would include foster-care services, rehabilitation programs for deliquent youth and drug abusers, and numerous counseling facilities—services, in other words, that modify behaviour or help those unable to assist themselves. Such programs are generally delivered directly by the federal government or by local governments with federal assistance, often through contracts with private nonprofit organizations.

The programs in the third category are not human services in a strict sense, but they are designed to assist low-income people in an indirect way. These include the numerous economic-development and job-creation programs that figure in the budgets of many federal departments, such as Urban Development Action Grants and the activities of the Economic Development Administration. These programs spend money on various projects, with the aim of stimulating economic development and job creation.

As we shall see, public spending coalitions are a powerful force behind the growth of human-services programs. Because the beneficiaries of this spending are low-income people, resistance to spending growth is a politically sensitive issue, and so the privatization strategy must be designed very carefully. In addition, the growth of human-services spending illustrates the considerable drawbacks of contracting out as a version of privatization. Private nonprofit organizations delivering human services have become a potent element of the public spending coalition. In the matter of health services, effectively removing the keystone of the private market price from the decision-making process has added to this spending pressure from service providers by removing the incentive to economize.

The task confronting the privatizer of human services is thus by no means an easy one, but it is performable. By recognizing that the success of the spending coalition depends on the public's desire to help the disadvantaged to obtain federal assistance, the shape of a strategy begins to emerge. The privatizer must encourage the growth of new coalitions that can challenge the constituencies now supporting ballooning federal spending—coalitions that are plausible to the public, effective in delivering services, and inherently less costly to the taxpayer. This means shifting the decision-making power away from the producers of human services and into the hands of the consumers of those services.

A Low-Budget Great Society

Very early in his first term, Ronald Reagan acquired the reputation of a savage cutter of human-service programs. Dramatic White House victories during the 1981 congressional budget process seemed to many to indicate that a decisive change had taken place in the role of the federal government. Well-publicized individual cases of hardship have given the strong impression that federal assistance to the less fortunate has been cut back decisively and has not been replaced by other sources.

The impact of the administration's budget changes will be debated for many years to come, but studies analyzing the years 1981–83 suggest strongly that the financial effects were far less severe than is commonly supposed. A major study by the American Enterprise Institute, for instance, found that after dipping in 1982, real outlays resumed their upward trend in 1983.[2] Even this conclusion may be misleading, the study notes, because an important part of the administration's strategy involved targeting safety-net programs more effectively by tightening eligibility rules—concentrating more assistance on the needy by turning some beneficiaries into near-beneficiaries: "The administration's efforts to improve targeting have probably offset part if not all of the reductions, so that benefits actually going to the poor have not decreased as much as the outlay figure. In the case of food stamps, for example, the share of benefits going to the poor increased from 72% to 81% between 1980 and 1982."[3]

The net effect of the first Reagan administration's programs has been to create what some cynics have called a "low-budget Great Society," rather than to effect a radical restructuring of human services. In certain programs, such as housing and job training, some important first steps were taken in a new direction. But for the most part, the administration squeezed programs instead of reforming them, and simply resisted the underlying pressure for expansion instead of diverting it out of the public sector. The political dynamics that have driven these programs for decades remain intact.

The principal reason for the limited impact of Reagan's attempt to cut the human-services budget is that the administration has been unable to win further significant budget changes since 1981, or even to sustain all of those enacted in that first year. As opposition to the president's program consolidated after his early victories, Congress blocked further deep cuts and restored a substantial number of the cuts in grants-in-aid to the states.

A detailed study of Reagan policies by the Woodrow Wilson School of Princeton University indicates that the effects of federal cutbacks have also been offset to a great degree by state action to replace federal funds.[4] The study notes that the specter of federal cutbacks, combined with demands imposed by the 1981–82 recession, forced states to explore new ways of delivering basic services. State actions induced tax hikes, the imposition of user fees, and the reorganization of programs (the latter made more possible thanks to the new Reagan block grants): "In sum, as a result both of restoration and replacement actions, plus the unwillingness of Congress to continue to cut grant-in-aid spending after 1981, the momentum of the Reagan domestic program was significantly dissipated after 1981 in terms of its effects on state and local public finance and services."[5]

Despite the failure of its New Federalism initiative, therefore, the administration has still managed to move the responsibility for financing certain basic programs to the states—an important objective of the Reagan White House. Yet this top-down pressure on states does not seem to have moved the country far toward the Reagan ideal of a "good neighbor" society based on local communities caring for their own citizens. As John Herbers of *The New York Times* observed in his analysis of the Princeton study:

> Although [Reagan] has achieved a large measure of increased authority for the states and less for the national government, he has not effected the grass-roots control he had sought for local governments. The states have not passed their new powers along to the local level, nor has Mr. Reagan achieved the large reduction in federal financing that he advocated.
>
> What appears to have happened, according to both the Princeton study and other evidence, is that the various

interests that helped obtain the programs in Washington shifted their lobbying to the state level and have been more effective than was anticipated.[6]

In sum, the Reagan administration has acquired a reputation for budget-cutting effectiveness and meanness that it does not deserve. It is true that by attacking the supply of federal dollars, it has managed to shift some responsibilities to the states. This is welcome in itself, because moving programs down the federal ladder, causes them to be subjected to more assiduous voter scrutiny and thus forces them to reflect more accurately the taxpayers' wishes. But these modest changes were achieved only after intense and damaging political effort, and they have since been diluted by congressional action.

The administration has failed entirely to change the underlying political dynamics that generate the demand for federal spending on such programs. So there is little reason to suppose that the cuts will survive for long—especially if the political complexion of the government becomes more liberal after the 1988 election. Unless the new administration can alter the demand side of the equation, the Reagan "cuts" will constitute no more than a temporary blip in the trend line of accelerating social spending.

The Dynamics of Human Service Spending

Program Expansion

The public spending coalitions discussed in Chapter 1 have proved particularly formidable in expanding and preserving human-service programs. Beneficiaries and near-beneficiaries, in cooperation with service providers, political activists, and administrators of programs, have managed to maintain the momentum generated during the Johnson administration. They have succeeded in widening the scope of federal departments, and they have successfully defended the bulk of programs from attack by fiscal conservatives.

The coalitions have used a number of methods to build up public support for extensions of federal human-service programs. Research and advocacy, often funded by the federal government itself, have been key factors in lobbying efforts for federal programs. Each issue of *The Federal Register* is packed with announcements of grants for research and demonstration projects, reflecting the objectives of program administrators. Given that those who choose a career in the federal government generally favor federal solutions to problems, and given that researchers or contractors seeking government work have little incentive to disillusion career officials, it is common for a close working relationship to develop.

James Bovard has observed this interaction in the workings of federal food programs.[7] The steady expansion of food assistance eligibility (and thus spending), he alleges, was the result of a conscious campaign to make the federal government responsible for basic food requirements; it did not arise from an evident need for federal spending on the scale demanded. He notes that in 1955, the U.S. Department of Agriculture found that only 25% of America's 40 million poor had bad diets—even though two-thirds received little or no public assistance. Between 1963 and 1966, *The New York Times* did not run a single article on hunger in America, says Bovard, yet by the late 1960s an impression had been created by advocates of the Great Society that hunger was rampant and that it could be cured only by federal spending of crisis proportions. By the 1970s, officials at the Agriculture Department and the Community Services Administration were funding food advocacy organizations, which in turn urged extensions of food assistance coverage. Despite a lack of firm evidence that hunger was growing in the United States, such agency-sponsored campaigns, aided by increasing media coverage of the "hunger crisis," have resulted in federal food-assistance spending now approaching $20 billion a year.

The courts have also become an increasingly attractive vehicle for advocacy organizations trying to force more spending. For instance, notes education analyst Eileen Gardner, proponents of the view that the federal government should take greater responsibility for the education of handicapped children have made skillful use of civil rights laws to require publicly supported education for the handicapped, regardless of the costs it imposes on government.[8]

Thanks to the general public's sympathy toward human-services programs, the coalitions backing such programs have been successful at defending them against major cutbacks or restructuring. They have managed this despite the political weakness of the primary beneficiaries, and even when the effectiveness or necessity of the program is in serious question. Once the programs are in place, they are very difficult to end or to reform. There is little evidence, for instance, to show that the creation of the federal Department of Education has helped improve educational standards. Much evidence in fact demonstrates an inverse relationship between federal spending and academic performance. Yet Ronald Reagan's 1980 pledge to abolish the department is no longer even taken seriously. Similarly, when the Reagan administration, in 1983, proposed changes in the regulation supplementing the Education for All Handicapped Children Act designed to reduce the cost, lobbyists bitterly attacked the rule changes during emotional and well-publicized hearings, and the administration and its congressional supporters were forced to back down.

The Reagan administration stepped into even hotter political water in 1983, when White House counselor Edwin Meese III ventured the opinion that there were no "authoritative figures" on which to base the theory that hunger remains wide-spread in America. Although persuasive national figures were not forthcoming, outraged critics of the administration expressed disbelief that the White House should even question the "fact" of extensive hunger. "We cannot tell you the exact number of hungry people in the United States," said an angry Mayor Richard Fulton of Nashville. "Nobody can. But that doesn't mean they aren't there."[9] When the administration tried to defuse the situation by appointing a panel to investigate hunger, and when that task force also found the evidence inconclusive, its findings were buried in hostile reaction, including a joint denunciation by forty-two national antipoverty and religious organizations.

Crowding Out Competitors

Federal human-services programs do not grow and resist cutbacks only because their constituent interest groups can mobilize media support and exert political pressure. They also grow large and expensive because professional providers of those services have been able to replace, or crowd out, lower-cost alternative service delivery groups at least as competent as the professional organizations.

To understand how service providers can accomplish this, it is important to appreciate the close relationship between government and the "voluntary" sector. The federal government makes extensive use of private nonprofit organizations in providing human services—so much so that Urban Institute scholar Lester Salamon describes the practice as "third party government."

Federal money flows in three broad ways, notes Salamon. The least common involves direct federal assistance to nonprofit organizations (about 20% of all federal cash to nonprofit outfits was distributed in this way in FY 1980). The second form is indirect assistance through state and local government (27% in FY 1980), where

Table 4

Nonprofit Revenues from Federal and Private Sources, FY 1980
(in billions of dollars)

Type of Organization	Total Revenues	Federal Programs as Percent of Total
Social Service	$13.2	8
Community Development	5.4	43
Education and Research	15.2	22
Health Care	70.0	36
Arts and Culture	2.6	12

Source: Lester M. Salamon and Alan Abramson, *The Federal Budget and the Nonprofit Sector* (Washington, D.C.: Urban Institute), p. 44.

the money comes from Washington but is administered by lower tiers of government. The third and most common route (53% in FY 1980) is through individuals or financial agents acting on their behalf. This last form would include such programs as college student assistance and Medicaid wherein the individual decides which nonprofit organization will receive the federal money.[10] Federal assistance has become an extremely important source of revenue for the nonprofit sector. The nonprofit health-care industry, for example, receives $70 billion a year from the federal government, and federal sources provide more than half of the revenues of social service organizations.

Salamon notes that this dependency on the federal government has occasioned three principal concerns. The first of these centers on the question of whether organizations lose their independence once they become "agents" of the government. Salamon believes that this threat has been exaggerated, especially when one remembers that an organization dependent on private funding is also by no means independent of its donors. The second concern, observes Salamon, involves the possibility that government funding may induce organizations to distort their activities simply to fit government programs. But, says Salamon, the empirical evidence suggests that federal funding has not altered the mission of nonprofit organizations but has allowed them to carry out chosen objectives for which alternative funding proved to be difficult to raise.

The third concern identified by Salamon centers on the contention that the red tape and controls associated with government funding encourage bureaucratization and professionalism among nonprofit organizations, reducing their reliance on local volunteer staff. Of all the potential problems related to government funding, concedes Salamon, this is the one most thoroughly supported by the evidence. Nevertheless, he argues, these pressures do not come solely from government; they reflect greater demands from all sources for better financial management. They reflect also the increased sophistication of the nonprofit sector.[11]

While they may agree in part with Salamon's assessment, other analysts are less sanguine, arguing that the real question is whether the tail wags the dog. In other words, does the close relationship between nonprofit organizations and the government mean that service providers have too much influence on policy and service delivery?

Salamon's surveys of nonprofit organizations, for instance, reveal that many of them favor government support because they find it hard to raise private finance for their chosen objectives. But the very independence that government support gives to nonprofit organizations causes concern to neighborhood experts such as Robert Woodson, president of the National Center for Neighborhood Enterprise. When organizations become independent of those whom they are supposed to assist, and have less need to justify their action to volunteers or private donors, says Woodson, the result is bad programs:

> The failure of many government programs can be traced to the underlying premise that centrally designed programs could be "parachuted" into poor neighborhoods and implemented by community action agencies *created by government*. This approach has resulted in a dependency relationship that is regarded even by the poor themselves as unworkable and inherently undesirable.[12]

Moreover, Woodson argues, the observation of Salamon and others that government funding allows nonprofit organizations greater freedom to choose their mission, merely results in

> a seller's market in that professionals themselves decide when, to whom, and how to serve. The result too often is the paradox of careless care, leading many of the poor to conclude that they must be saved from their champions. . . . Since professionals also control the criteria of professional success and the definition of its categories of

clients and their needs, professional services can survive any malfeasance and continue in business, unlike a friendship, a family, or even a true market enterprise. Professionals themselves determine whether they have succeeded or failed and, if the latter, what the remedy should be.[13]

Federal financing of nonprofit service providers, in other words, allows them greater power to determine what services shall be provided and reduces the pressure on them to be sensitive to local demands or to keep service costs down. Moreover, as Woodson argues, it means that in many instances the taxpayer is financing activities that achieve the objectives of the professionals running the nonprofit organization, yet are of little or no benefit to the people they are presumed to assist. Not surprisingly, the more important government funding has become for nonprofit outfits, the more effort and money they have devoted—including federal grant money itself—to lobbying for increased funding for human services. Such organizations have become a key pressure group for the creation of new federal programs and the retention of existing ones. The Independent Sector, an umbrella group for nonprofit organizations, has become an effective advocate for the whole sector. And service agencies have become highly adept at influencing the political process in Washington. In many instances these agencies led successful campaigns to block Reagan budget cuts.

Bureaucratization and professionalization may pose an even greater problem. Like all professions, nonprofit service providers have a financial interest in convincing the public that they alone are capable of providing a desired service, and that lower-cost but "unqualified" alternative providers are unsuitable. Wary of any challenge to their authority, the professionals press government to erect licensing barriers against their competitors. As sociologists Peter Berger and Richard Neuhaus put it,

> Whether in government or nongovernment agencies, professionals attack allegedly substandard services, and substandard generally means nonprofessional. Through organizations and lobbies, professionals increasingly persuade the state to legislate standards and certifications that hit voluntary associations hard, especially those given to employing volunteers. The end result is that the trend toward professional monopoly operates in tandem with the trend toward professional monopoly over social services. The connection between such monopoly control and the actual quality of services delivered is doubtful indeed.[14]

Such licensing and credentialing barriers pervade the human-services sector. Reasonable standards to protect people from unscrupulous or incompetent service providers is one thing, but licensing has slowly become a method of limiting the public's access to better services. Certification for teachers, for example, has angered parent organizations for years, as they see certified teachers in schools who know little subject matter, while highly effective teachers are deemed unqualified by teachers' unions. And at the same time the National Education Association demands more federal money to bridge the science gap, it continues to lobby for licensing procedures that prevent many knowledgeable industry experts from entering the classroom.

Day-care centers in private homes also face the considerable barriers of credentialing and facility licensing, despite their popularity with parents. So costs rise and pressures mount for more federal support for working mothers.[15] Adoption and foster-care services are so entwined with regulations to maintain "standards," says Woodson, that children are routinely kept in professionally run institutions at enormous cost to taxpayers, instead of being placed in private homes with caring families. Approximately 70% of the $2 billion spent by federal, state, and local governments on foster care each year, he says, is spent on professional salaries and administrative costs.[16] A 1981 audit of the District of Columbia's foster-care program, for instance, showed that institutionalization had become "a permanent way of life" for more than two thousand children. The audit indicated that the cost of keeping a foster child in an institution from age of 3 to 19 exceeds $120,000, and the annual rate for an infant at one institution was $12,775. When a child was placed with a foster family, on the other hand, the family received only $3,306.[17]

The result of these barriers is that in many services paid professionals have merely replaced volunteers, and centrally designed programs have crowded out unorthodox but highly effective local initiatives. Often the taxpayer ends up paying a great deal of money to deliver inferior human services. And professional service providers, in conjunction with legislators, have created many programs that not only encourage dependency on professional organizations, but sometimes actually exacerbate the social problems they were supposed to cure.

Corrupting the Private Sector

In addition to cost-increasing incentives resulting from the professionalization of the nonprofit sector, other forces drive up the cost of services. The virtual elimination of price in the health-care market, for instance, has removed normal price sensitivity and encouraged the overuse of high-cost procedures. The blame for this cannot be laid solely at the feet of those who designed the Medicaid and Medicare programs. The problem exists in large part because the private health-care industry is almost a private parallel to the public choice imbalance endemic to the federal spending process.

Individuals generally provide themselves with group health insurance to protect them from the sudden calamity of high medical bills. By so doing, they also effectively insulate themselves from the immediate cost of care by spreading the cost of their treatment over all those who have insurance, just as the cost of programs benefiting small groups is spread over all taxpayers. In addition, most insured workers are partly insulated from even this burden because they belong to tax-free group plans. Consequently, patients have much less incentive to question the cost of procedures than they would have if they faced the full cost of treatment—and the doctor has every incentive to provide patients with the best treatment available, virtually without regard to cost. Since the price system exerts little check on health costs, it should be no surprise that medical bills have been escalating more rapidly than price increases in most other areas of the economy.

Until very recently, notes American Enterprise Institute scholar Jack Meyer, such tax-supported third-party payments have driven up the cost of federally assisted health care, because "Federal reimbursement policies under Medicare and Medicaid were characterized both by generous retrospective cost-based payments to doctors and hospitals that rewarded inefficiency, and by a penurious stance toward care in non-institutional settings."[18] The cost to the federal government of these two programs has been doubling about every four years, and now constitutes approximately one dollar in every ten spent by the federal government.[19]

The staggering cost escalation of federal health-care costs demonstrates all too clearly the drawbacks of a simplistic attitude to contracting out. Merely inviting the private sector to provide services on demand and then to send Uncle Sam the bill is no way to reduce federal spending. The Reagan administration has taken the first steps toward building one requirement of effective contracting out—competition—by establishing a prospective payment system for hospital reimbursement under Medicare. Medicare will henceforth make payments according to fixed-payment rules for more than four hundred diagnostically related groups (DRG) of illnesses, instead of on a cost-plus basis. So hospitals now at least have a competitive profit-related motive to keep costs down.

Unfortunately, as Meyer notes, the complexity and lack of patient incentives will reduce the impact of the change. Moreover, until the tax-driven demand pressure from the private market is reduced, spillover costs will continue to be borne by the Medicaid and Medicare programs. In the matter of health care, demand pressure is still the principal ingredient in the cost equation.

Privatizing Human Services

The experience of the first Reagan administration vividly illustrated the diminishing political returns associated with a supply-side strategy designed to cut spending by denying federal funds to those who had grown accustomed to receiving them. After the initial successes of David Stockman's budget *blitzkrieg*, the public spending coalitions consolidated their position and conducted a successful war of attrition against the administration. Using the anger of beneficiaries cut from programs, relying on countless studies showing the horrors that would accompany a reduced federal role, and evoking the sympathy of the American people, the human-services industry conducted a campaign that fought the White House to a standstill. Since 1981, Reagan has achieved very little in the way of human-service spending reduction.

There is little reason to believe that attempts to reduce the flow of federal funds will be any more successful in the foreseeable future. After the shock of 1981, the coalitions are well entrenched. The only way the new administration stands any chance of achieving a significant and durable change in the role of the federal government is by changing the underlying political dynamics through a privatization strategy. To accomplish this the administration must do three things: (1) it must establish firmly in the minds of the public a view of community and obligation that is a plausible alternative to the liberal view; (2) it must identify and mobilize coalitions around that alternative; and (3) it must embark on a course of action that will strengthen those coalitions while weakening the existing public spending constituencies.

Setting the Tone of the Campaign

In 1981 President Reagan spent a great deal of time lauding voluntarism. He even set up a presidential task force to promote it. Yet other than providing a number of worthy organizations with the recognition they deserve and pressuring corporations to give away more of their stockholders' money, the effort has had minimal results. In particular, little has been done to develop an understandable and workable model of a civilized, caring society that makes much sense to the average voter and provides a sound foundation for policy.

If the advocates of smaller government are to win support for an alternative model, they must make a bid for the moral high ground by attacking the foundation of the liberal argument for an extensive federal role—the notion of a national community. As William Schambra explains, "the essential moral underpinning for liberalism's extensive federal social service program is 'the great national community'—the citizen's sense of belonging to one nation, and the feeling of obligation to help fellow citizens by means of national programs."[20] But, he points out, the flaw in this foundation is that Americans tend to think in terms of a national community, with every man and woman a neighbor, only on extraordinary occasions such as in a time of national danger, or at the behest of extraordinary leaders such as Lincoln or Franklin Roosevelt. "Each liberal president," observes Schambra, "must cast about for a 'moral equivalent of war.'"[21] The idea of a national community begins to fade rapidly in the minds of Americans if no such equivalent can be found.

Americans clearly *do* feel a strong sense of commitment to tangible local communities, however, and to the people and institutions within them such as family and church. These associations and institutions have a meaning and importance to Americans that a "national community" does not, and they stimulate a sense of obligation to neighbors that is rarely felt for distant citizens. Moreover, the associations that form within local communities have their roots in those communities. They must justify themselves to the residents if they are to survive, and their members have a strong self-interest in addressing effectively the crises or opportunities confronting the neighborhood. They are not like organizations consisting of outsiders and funded by outsiders—groups that enter a community because they have a federal contract to help people.

Local institutions and associations—or "mediating structures," as Berger and Neuhaus call them—are generally the avenue of first preference when the citizen needs help. Yet these institutions have been elbowed out of the way by the professionalized, federally funded, and detached organizations that owe their creation and continued existence to the liberal view of a national community. The idea of a welfare system based on such mediating structures would strike a strong chord in most Americans—a system encouraged by the federal government but not replaced by it, and supported by professionals who are, one might say, on tap, not on top. "The form of obligation thus nurtured [by the idea of such local private initiatives]," writes Schambra,

> is not, to be sure, the exalted, selfless kind that liberals prefer. It is modest—but it is enduring. It in fact rests on the ordinary, everyday circumstances of local administration and citizenly participation therein. In short, we have some hope that private sector initiatives will begin to rebuild the sense of community in America, because the democratic devices described by Tocqueville seek to nurture a form of public spiritedness or social obligation that is appropriate to the American regime. Liberalism's devices do not.[22]

The foundation of this new view of human services (or, rather, the revival of the original American view) rests on two notions: the idea that social obligation is a product of small communities, even if they are helped by state or national government; and the idea that freedom of choice, not participation in a system imposed from outside, should characterize the relationship between beneficiaries and the systems that assist them.

Peter Berger calls this model of social services "empowerment." This means treating people as consumers, in contrast with the national welfare-state model, which, he says, treats them as passive "clients." Extending on this basic distinction, Berger puts forward four criteria that should characterize a system based on empowerment[23]:

> 1. Government should empower people to take control of their own lives even as it provides services to meet specific needs. Or minimally: government should not, in providing services, take away such control as people do have over their lives.

Government and its institutions, says Berger, thus should not, for example, force parents to give up their rights and responsibilities in exchange for educating their children. When it provides education through a public school system not of the parents' choosing, affluent parents can always escape it. It is poor people who are subjected to "a coercive monopoly."

> 2. As far as possible, recipients of government-supplied social services should have a choice between suppliers. Put differently: As far as possible, suppliers of social services should be forced to compete with each other for the favor of recipients.[24]

Monopolies corrupt, notes Berger, while the freedom to choose turns clients into powerful consumers. The freedom to take one's child to another school, for instance, provides a far greater guarantee of quality and efficiency for each parent than any amount of representative "participation."

3. Those who provide social services should be accountable to those who receive the services.[25]

There is nothing anti-professional or even anti-bureaucratic in this criterion, says Berger. Rather, the intent is to make professionals exercise their talents "in the service of independent and uncoerced people, instead of making people the passive objects of professional and bureaucratic ministrations."

4. Social policy should respect the pluralism of values and life-styles in American society.[26]

Social policy should draw on the diversity of American society and build on the strengths of diverse cultures. It should not "impose on everyone the values and life-styles established in the white, college-educated, upper middle class."

The implication of these criteria is that mediating structures, those institutions that stand between the state and the individual (such as church, family, and neighborhood groups), should be the centerpiece of the new model of the welfare state. Before the creation of the modern welfare state, explains Berger, all social services were provided by institutions of this kind. America should not go back to that time, and dismantle all means of providing financial and other assistance by government, but government programs and their constituencies should not be allowed to cripple or destroy mediating structures.

> The state should not needlessly duplicate what mediating structures are doing: This means taking cognizance of all the private initiatives in play, and the planning of state actions *around*, and not *against* them. Also it means that the state should not inhibit these private initatives by foolish and unnecessary regulation.[27]

Yet it is not enough, insists Berger, for government merely to keep out of the way. It must do what it can to create an environment conducive to such freely chosen social service structures—not by picking and choosing among them but by empowering the consumers of services to make that choice. This can be accomplished by social deregulation, he argues, which would allow new structures to emerge, and by stimulating "consumer power." The latter can be encouraged by means of grants, tax incentives, and vouchers in such a way that social service providers would be forced to become sensitive to those whom they serve rather than to the politics of Washington.

This is the essence of privatizing human services. By shifting financial power into the hands of service consumers, and by breaking the effective monopoly enjoyed by many current service providers, a privatization strategy would subtly alter the political dynamics of service provision, leading to a shift in emphasis toward lower-cost locally based organizations *preferred* by beneficiaries, and away from high-cost professionalized organizations *imposed* on them. In short, privatization enables budget cutters to unflank the human services "industry" by reducing spending as they allow beneficiaries the right to choose the provider who shall help them.

Identifying Privatization Coalitions

The human-service industry is not given to inviting competition. It has every incentive to ridicule the idea that effective alternatives to it exist, and it has shown its ability in the past to undermine competition. If the administration were simply to invite private organizations to make themselves available to provide assistance, little would change because the existing public spending coalitions are visible and well entrenched and their potential competitors are not. Before privatization can succeed, therefore, these alternative sources of assistance must be identified and their potential made clear to the public. They must be made more visible to the voter, and they must be mobilized into a political force.

The shape of some possible privatization coalitions is relatively easy to discern, whereas the shape of others is less obvious. Middle-class parents, for instance, have long been supporters of tuition tax credits, vouchers, and other mechanisms to stimulate private alternatives to public education. So far such pressure has been blocked by the National Education Association and its allies, who argue that such mechanisms would merely give freedom and benefits to the rich. Often overlooked, however, have been the growth of minority enrollment in private schools and, even more important, the acceptance of inner-city private schools for the children of low-income families.

Black and Hispanic enrollment in Catholic elementary and secondary schools jumped from 9.8% to 16.4% between 1970 and 1980, for instance, and Gallup poll data consistently show that the highest rate of dissatisfaction with urban public schools is found among inner-city blacks.[28] And many low-income minorities opting out of the public schools are not merely content with sending their children to church-affiliated schools. In a preliminary survey, the National Center for Neighborhood Enterprise has identified 250 independent neighborhood schools, chiefly in urban communities, that cater to low-income minority families. The study team believes that the number of such schools in existence is several times the number actually identified and examined.[29] Mainly established in the 1960s and early 1970s, these schools not only pay close attention to basic skills that are inadequately taught in the public schools, but they also tend to lay great emphasis on reinforcing the cultural, religious, and ethnic roots of the local community. As survey director Joan Ratteray puts it,

> many parents of poor and minority children are controlling the education of their children by choosing neighborhood-based private schools. They are enrolling their children in private schools that operate almost exclusively on tuition and modest community fundraising—often at great financial sacrifice—using welfare checks, depending on family and friends for tuition, by working multiple jobs or using weekends to supplement educational objectives.[30]

These schools began, for the most part, because of the efforts of parents and teachers who were dissatisfied with the quality of education provided by urban public schools. They have been able to continue because of strong community backing in the form of financial and volunteer help—and often despite credentialing and code challenges by antagonistic local governments and public school systems. When asked how the federal government could help them, school officials cite one thing above all else—vouchers. Vouchers, they say, would relieve the enormous financial burden on the parents of existing students and enable many more low-income parents to escape the public school monopoly. They would permit these schools to compete head to head with the public sector.

Clearly the National Center for Neighborhood Enterprise has uncovered a powerful constituency for the education voucher proposal—one that the Reagan administration has completely overlooked. The parents and staff of minority-operated inner-city private schools could become key components of the coalition for achieving, through education vouchers, a privatized alternative to low-quality but expensive public schools.

In general, local organizations in low-income communities appear to be an enormous, but largely untapped, resource for the provision of more effective human services at much lower cost. They shatter the stereotype of the volunteer—the suburban housewife collecting for the Red Cross—and their roots in poor communities mean they can approach social problems with unconventional but successful methods.

David and Falaka Fattah, for instance, tackled the youth gang warfare that plagued west Philadelphia in the 1960s by opening up their own home as a safe haven for gang members who had grown sick of the death and pointless destruction. The Fattahs combined tough discipline with the positive bonds of the extended family to redirect the lives of the young men. The results have been dramatic. Largely thanks to the Fattahs and their House of Umoja project, the number of gang-related deaths in west Philadelphia has fallen from forty a year to one a year.

The Fattahs and the former gang leaders recognized that long-term solutions to neighborhood problems would come only through economic growth, and that businesses and jobs could be created only if companies, residents, and workers felt safe. So Umoja has now set up a security service, which has helped to revive commerce in the area. Some members have worked to create their own businesses.

Even professional organizations recognize the success of the House of Umoja, and the Philadelphia juvenile courts now send their worst cases to Umoja for care. As a measure of Umoja's effectiveness, the Philadelphia Psychiatric Center, in a survey of recidivism, found that the re-arrest rate of ex-offenders at Umoja was just 3% compared with up to 87% at some "correctional" facilities in the city.[31]

Similar successes have been achieved by nonprofessional organizations in other low-income communities. Professional foster-care specialists in Detroit, for instance, used to maintain that black families were not interested in adoption, and so they placed most of their black children with white families or in expensive institutions. But a community-based group decided to challenge the city's adoption practices. In its first year, Homes for Black Children placed far more black children with black families than all thirteen of Detroit's placement agencies put together. The group's effectiveness has forced the professional agencies to use many of the same techniques employed by Homes for Black Children.[32]

Successful community-based initiatives such as these have become increasingly common in low-income neighborhoods as residents grow disillusioned with programs designed by specialists who have no commitment to the neighborhood. In the provision of day care, job training, help for the elderly, economic development work, and many other activities, neighborhood organizations have shown themselves able to deliver services less extensively and more effectively than professional service providers. As *The New York Times* noted in a 1983 report on urban services, financial pressures have encouraged city halls around the nation to ignore union opposition and turn to neighborhood organizations to provide and manage such services as social service centers, shelters for the poor, parks, housing rehabilitation, assistance for the disabled, drug treatment centers, recreation programs, crime prevention patrols, and even building inspections: "Such delegations of authority, unheard of in the past, are writing the latest chapter in the fast-evolving role of neighborhood groups and in the 'privatization' of local governments. Part of this trend is that neighborhood groups are becoming more formally organized and entrepreneurial."[33]

Unlike governments at the state and local level, which are for the most part its ideological opponents, the first Reagan administration did very little to draw on the lessons of the phenomenon of human-services privatization at the local level. It failed to appreciate the political implications of the natural tension that exists between such groups and the professional service industry. Consequently, Reagan officials also overlooked the possibility that these organizations could form the base of a privatization coalition against the powerful lobbies now dominating social service budgeting in Washington. Instead, the Reagan administration has generally seen such organizations in one of two lights. Some officials saw them as a threat, based on their memories of community activists in the 1960s and 1970s; others thought of them as token partners in private-sector initiatives—in which corporate altruism is the driving force and downtown executives make all the important decisions.

Given this myopic attitude, it is unlikely that the full potential of the human-services privatization coalition will be realized unless perceptive officials take some important steps to mobilize these alternative service providers. In the first place, no coalition can be assembled until its possible members are known. As a result of its survey, the National Center for Neighborhood Enterprise learned that many private schools in low-income areas had no knowledge of the existence of schools in other cities. The same is often true of other local service organizations. So considerable research needs to be undertaken to discover this "underground" system of providers. But the research responsibility cannot be entrusted to the agencies and research organizations within the existing formal structure of human services. That would be rather like asking the fox to count the chickens. The task must be given to organizations outside the Washington orbit—organizations that have a knowledge of neighborhoods.

Second, the limits of altruism and "public-private partnerships" have to be understood in assessing the role of business support. The liberal notion of a national community is seriously flawed. But so is the idea that large corporations have some national affinity for all volunteer efforts and should therefore be willing to support welfare mothers just as enthusiastically as they fund the opera. This view figured strongly in the recommendations of the 1981–82 President's Task Force on Private Sector Initiatives. These led the administration to suggest, in effect, that corporations should take over some responsibility for funding professional nonprofit organizations hit by federal budget cuts. Not surprisingly, this suggestion was eagerly endorsed by those organizations.

Calls for checkbook support from corporations overlook the nature of corporate philanthropy, which reflects a perceived, and quite proper, "community of interest" on the part of the corporation. Private firms have good reasons to support research, job-training programs, or cultural activities that enhance their corporate reputation among key constituencies. Corporations have good reason, also, to invest in major urban revitalization projects when they are likely to see a tangible payoff in the form of economic growth. Such business-supported ventures, where private ends are served by contributions to public projects, are in the best American tradition of community development.[34] By contrast, the suggestion that corporations do, or should, have some inate desire to assist all who need help demonstrates a fundamental misunderstanding of the concept of community.

A final point about building coalitions of alternative service providers must also be appreciated if privatization is to be successful: When funding becomes important, the manner in which it is made available is critical. Many a successful local organization has been destroyed when government—or a large private foundation, for that matter—decided to help it. External top-down funding brings with it rules and regulations that foster bureaucratization and professionalization. Moreover, once an organization is made financially independent of the community it was formed to serve, it becomes less sensitive to community needs. This danger is implicit in contracting out as well as grant-making. Unless "consumers" continue to pull the financial levers, as Peter Berger explained in his list of criteria for a new model of social services, it is hard to ensure that service providers will remain innovative, economical, and community-sensitive.

A Plan of Action

Given the alternative model for human services put forward by Berger and others, and the requirements for coalition building discussed above, the political strategy to reduce social spending through privatization becomes more apparent. The strategy should be based on encouraging the emergence of lower-cost competitors to existing providers, and on changing the financing method for human services in such a way as to increase the power of service consumers. In short, the strategy should attempt to weaken the provider-led coalitions, which have the incentive to increase costs without improving quality, while strengthening consumer-led coalitions that have the incentive to be sensitive to beneficiary interest.

1. Undertake research to identify alternative providers and encourage them to form networks

The administration and privately supported institutions should also undertake research projects whose aim is to identify alternative human-service providers and the barriers they face. In awarding such research grants, the administration should adopt a conscious policy of bypassing the cozy research network that has developed around current federal programs. A base of government-supported research institutions is important to the consolidation of political coalitions: The administration must seek to develop that research base for privatization coalitions while denying it to the public spending coalitions.

Data from research should also be used to help alternative providers organize their own networks. This step is essential for two reasons. First, groups need to learn from one another's experiences. The more efficient the information flow between groups, the quicker they can adapt and the stronger they will become. And second, it is difficult for groups of providers to exercise political clout if they are not organized into networks. The coalitions supporting existing federal programs are highly organized, with sophisticated channels of communication and lobbying capacity. For privatization to succeed, rival networks need to be formed by such means as bringing together groups through conferences and establishing national headquarters.

2. Attack regulatory barriers

When needless licensing and other regulatory barriers to alternative providers are identified, they should be challenged and removed whenever possible. This is no simple objective, since such regulations protect the interests of the providers, who justify them to the general public by claiming that they are needed to uphold standards. Consequently, challenges to these regulatory barriers need to be mounted in coordination with other actions designed to win public support.

Privatizers might use various methods to do this. One would be to borrow some of the techniques of the public-sector coalitions. Activists such as Ralph Nader have used legal action with devastating effect to expose special interests and deficiencies within the private sector and thus win public support for "remedies" involving more government. Litigating organizations favoring smaller government could act on behalf of local service providers, such as home-based day-care centers and neighborhood private schools that are threatened by special-interest regulation. Legal challenges would draw public attention to the unreasonableness of many rules and show that those barriers are designed to shut out lower-cost competitors preferred by community residents. This way the privatizers could put the current providers on the defensive. Legal challenges could also lead to regulations that genuinely protect the recipients of services rather than the providers.

Aided by such public discussion, the administration could then move to change regulations affecting federal spending programs, and to reduce professionalization by liberalizing rules governing the credentials of service providers. The cost of the services to be provided, and evidence of financial and volunteer support within the community, should be given greater weight instead in the awarding of contracts. Pressure should also be applied to the states to encourage similar changes in credentialing and licensing rules at that level of government, perhaps by seeking riders to that effect on legislation authorizing grants to states.

3. Reform tax incentives

As explained in Chapter 2, tax incentives are vital to the privatization approach. They can influence demand decisions by providing a concentrated benefit on key constituencies, giving them a financial interest in seeing private-sector alternatives become established and flourish. In the matter of human services, however, the usefulness of this technique is clearly limited. Needy people assisted by federal programs pay little or no income tax, and so tax incentives are unlikely to cause them to change their preferences. Tax incentives can be used, however, to encourage taxpayers to give financial support to nongovernmental providers of services. They can be effective, in other words, in concentrating "benefits" on people who discharge their social responsibility in this way by increasing the cash value of their after-tax contributions.

The current charitable deduction, of course, provides such an incentive. But it does have drawbacks. Because it is a deduction and not a credit, it gives the greatest incentive to high-income Americans and the least to low-income people supporting community initiatives. Until changes recently were legislated into the tax code, few working-class Americans could enjoy any tax benefit at all for charitable donations, since tax relief was available only to those who itemize their deductions. An "above-the-line" deduction, however, is now being phased in.

To make the tax incentive equal among income groups, it has been widely suggested that the charitable deduction should be converted to a tax credit, to give all Americans the same marginal incentive to donate. Given the normal patterns of giving, religious organizations would gain most from that change. A serious tax-credit proposal would no doubt encounter heavy opposition from the health and cultural sectors, which are favored more by high-income taxpayers.[35] But a small above-the-line credit in addition to tax deductibility limited to gifts to health and social service providers would meet less resistance while stimulating contributions to such institutions among middle- and lower-income taxpayers.

If the enormous human-services budget is to be reduced, however, opening up opportunities for alternative social service organizations will not be enough. Something will have to be done about health. As noted earlier, the cost of health care for the poor has been inflated because federal tax policy has increased the price of care by excessively subsidizing to demand (by making employer-paid plans tax free without limit) and by providing retrospective reimbursement. Some steps have been taken to tackle the problem of reimbursement, but the Reagan administration's attempts to place a cap on the deductibility of health insurance have met a wall of opposition from business organizations and organized labor, both of which wish to retain the tax-free benefit for bargaining purposes.

Ironically, the unwillingness of Congress to limit this tax incentive is testimony to the political power of a privatization coalition formed around a tax break. The problem is that in this instance privatization has worked so well that there is now overdemand and cost escalation. Perhaps the only way to redirect these incentives, as Jack Meyer suggests, is to link a cap on the insurance deduction with a program to use the tax revenue obtained to provide assistance for the poorest Americans to buy insurance.[36] This would reduce the upward price pressure due to demand subsidies for the middle and upper class, thereby reducing costs for federal health-care assistance programs. It could also be a politically effective proposal, since it would give advocates for the poor a good reason to join in a challenge to the tax-free status of company-based health plans.

The use of tax incentives to encourage the private support of service providers differs in important ways from direct federal support. In the first place, tax incentives are less expensive to government, since the tax relief is less than the amount contributed to the service provider. But second, and more important, the use of tax incentives means that decisions regarding financial support are made by private individuals and firms using their own money, and not by government officials using sombody else's. This in turn means that the choice of providers to be funded turns on the ability of those providers to convince private individuals that they are worthy of their support, and not on the lobbying power of the providers or on their compliance with federal guidelines.

The more successful the administration is in building privatization coalitions in these ways, the greater will be the chances of winning support for reductions in federal outlays for existing providers. In the meantime, federal departments should make every effort to redirect authorized funding to organizations that have been identified by research as more responsive to local needs. But in so doing, officials should be mindful of this danger: As such groups become less dependent on volunteers and local support, they may become more bureaucratized and less sensitive to the community. This privatization technique is not simply a matter of switching finance from one group to another, in other words, but of doing so in a way that preserves the recipient groups' characteristics. That means keeping assistance at low levels and tying it to strong evidence of community support.

4. Expand the use of vouchers

Although tax incentives are useful in stimulating support for alternative services, probably the most powerful mechanism available to change the pattern of supply is the voucher. It is most suitable for goods and services that are essentially private in nature, but which poor people cannot afford. A voucher enables the poor to enter the private marketplace and to exercise the same kind of consumer power as do affluent persons.

When individuals are provided with vouchers of fixed value, negotiable only for certain goods or services, they have the incentive to choose the supplier that meets their needs most efficiently. If the right to supply these services is fairly open, competitive pressures force suppliers to be sensitive to the consumers' needs—in stark contrast to the situation where suppliers are chosen and financed directly by government. When vouchers are the suppliers' means of income, effectiveness becomes more important than good relations with officials.[37] Peter Berger believes that the voucher concept is a basic ingredient for his model of a welfare state based on mediating structures. "Most people," he says, "if given a choice, will 'cash in' their vouchers at this or that mediating structure, either already in existence or newly set up to provide a particular service."[38]

Vouchers are not new; they have a good record of empowering low-income people or other targeted groups to obtain services in the private market. Analyses of voucher programs at the state and local level suggest that if the voucher amount is tied to the costs of the more efficient providers, competitive pressures will reduce total service costs.[39] Vouchers have been used for a wide range of local services. Despite the controversy over education vouchers at the national level, for instance, John McClaughry reports that one version of the voucher has been in operation for years in many Vermont towns.[40] And an Urban Institute survey of private service delivery notes that vouchers have been used to finance such privatized services as transportation for the elderly and handicapped, and day care for low-income families.[41]

Vouchers have been used much more extensively at the federal level, however. Food stamps and the WIC program (for pregnant women and new mothers) have done much to alleviate hunger among the poor, even if the eligibility criteria are highly questionable. Food stamps give the target population the same choice of private food outlets as a person of modest but independent means, and so avoid the need for a vast food-distribution network operated by the government. The G.I. Bill was also a form of voucher system. So is the targeted jobs tax credit for hard-to-employ individuals—although it has been less successful, chiefly because it is less widely known than other vouchers and because employers know that the eligible employees may perform less well than other workers. The Reagan administration has also won congressional approval for an experimental housing voucher program, in which low-income tenants receive allowances to enable them to rent units in the open market.

The Reagan administration has proposed extending the use of vouchers to three other services: educating disadvantaged children, providing Medicare benefits, and helping the long-term unemployed obtain work. Vouchers have been suggested for such diverse services as day care, health care, elementary and secondary education, clothing, vocational education, and technical assistance for neighborhood organizations. In each example the argument put forward is basically the same: Vouchers would empower low-income people to escape the straitjacket of public-sector monopolies, and would bring down costs through the power of competition.

Not surprisingly, advocates of the existing methods of federal financing are not exactly amenable to the idea of vouchers. The National Education Association has vehemently, and so far successfully, opposed education vouchers on the grounds that they would threaten the quality of education in the public schools the union controls—which is exactly why so many parents support vouchers. And lobbyists for service organizations now operating on government contracts generally maintain that standards of service would fall if low-income people were given the means to buy services in the marketplace—a common line of argument used by those who fear competition, and one that shows utter disdain for the common sense of poor people.

Although lobbyists have been able to defeat recent demands for wider use of vouchers at the federal level (with the exception of housing vouchers), the proposals do represent a political hot potato for the coalitions supporting the current system of services. They must maintain that monopoly is superior to competition and that low-income people are incapable of making rational choices. But if progress is made in identifying and mobilizing alternative providers, and if consumers of services are made more aware of them, Congress will find it increasingly difficult to oppose vouchers.

Yet the voucher mechanism does have its dangers. As the food stamp program has demonstrated, it can be very difficult to stop the spread of such entitlements to near-beneficiaries. There is little evidence, however, to suggest that vouchers are any more susceptible to such expansionary tendencies than are conventional programs. Indeed, since vouchers lead to a wider array of more competitive suppliers, coordinated lobbying by suppliers for increased funding is likely to be less of a problem than it is under the current arrangements. Nevertheless, expansion remains a danger as long as large amounts of money are involved, and so voucher programs must be designed with great care. One approach, however, could reduce expansionary pressure: Voucher programs could be funded at the federal level, and the broad eligibility guidelines could be established in Washington; but the money could be distributed in the form of grants to the states, which would then determine the exact eligibility standards. This procedure would encourage experimentation. It would also create state-government lobbies seeking to widen eligibility criteria. But each state would have to choose criteria in the knowledge that its total federal grant was fixed. If the state gave in to lobbying pressure, it would have to find the extra money itself; the funds would not come from taxes spread over the whole nation.

Recent attempts to reduce spending on human services have largely failed because they have sought only to deny services to people. The political difficulty and cost of pursuing such cuts has been immense, especially in light of the results actually achieved. The Reagan administration quickly discovered that trying to squeeze federal spending on human services just caused the political heat to rise. Since the underlying political dynamics were not altered, pressure mounted, and eventually the administration's congressional support gave way.

Privatization offers a budget-cutting administration the chance to change those dynamics and outflank the coalitions now dominating policy on human services. The strategy would enable the administration to capture the political high ground through a commitment to choice and the empowerment of poor people. It would hold open the probability that alternative coalitions would emerge to challenge those now in control. And by encouraging lower-cost alternatives to expensive social services, it would relieve spending pressure at the federal level. In short, privatization would enable the administration to spend less money by providing more opportunity.

5

FEDERAL SERVICES

In addition to providing a wide range of human services to groups of Americans who could be described as less fortunate, the federal government administers a host of programs that deliver benefits not particularly aimed at low-income groups. There are several reasons for this. One category of programs is intended to fulfill explicit social purposes identified by legislators. The National Endowment for the Arts and the Corporation for Public Broadcasting, for instance, were established to use public money to foster the arts and noncommercial broadcasting, on the grounds that this is good for society and yet the private sector fails to meet the need. Similarly, Congress provides over a billion dollars a year in subsidies to the U.S. Postal Service so as to maintain a universal mail service at a uniform price throughout the nation.

A second category of federal services consists of special research assistance that benefits primarily the business community. These programs rest on two contentions. Some, such as deep space exploration programs, are intended to finance and undertake primary research that has no immediate practical application and is beyond the resources of the academic community. If the federal government did not carry out such research, the argument goes, discoveries would not be made that prove to have unexpected and significant benefits to the nation. Another group of such programs stems from the claim that certain long-range economic enterprises are simply too large for the private sector to undertake, or the payoff is too distant to induce private investors to advance the necessary funds. Two examples of these in the energy field are the $13-billion Synthetic Fuels Corporation, designed to finance the development of non-petroleum forms of energy, and the now defunct Clinch River Breeder Reactor, a demonstration project for a new generation of nuclear reactors. Similarly, the ambitious space shuttle and space station programs are aimed, among other things, at spurring the commercialization of space by financing and developing the "infrastructure" of a space industry.

The third group of federal services could best be described as those that provide common-pool or collective goods; that is, goods and services that are jointly consumed and for which it is difficult or unreasonable to levy a charge. The most obvious and expensive example of such a service is national defense. Some would argue that this category of programs should also include services such as weather forecasting and the air traffic control system, on the grounds that these federal services indirectly benefit the entire nation and the private sector would be unable to provide them as effectively as the federal government does.

As in the matter of human services, however, the reality turns out to be substantially different from the theory used to support these federal activities. When services are provided directly by government employees, on the one hand, the interest of those employees invariably takes precedence over the public interest the programs are supposed to promote. When private firms bid to supply those goods and services, on the other hand, the public is likely to be better served. It should always be remembered, however, that the private sector is motivated to perform efficiently because of competition, not altruism. So when the government's own management structure is flawed—as in the Department of Defense, for instance—contracting out to private companies is no guarantee that goods and services will be produced according to reasonable standards of performance and price. And when the federal government offers to provide funding for long-term business research and development—but only if private-sector finance proves to be insufficient—it is remarkable how meager private funds suddenly become, and how diligently the private sector lobbies for research projects that allegedly benefit the nation.

Examples of these three categories of programs will be examined in this chapter. The U.S. Postal Service shows what can happen to costs and service quality when a government agency is given the exclusive responsibility to ensure that some social purpose is achieved. Experience suggests that privatization would allow that objective to be achieved at far less cost. The commercial space transportation program of the National Aeronautics and Space Administration (NASA), on the other hand, is supposed to meet a "deficiency" in the private market by guaranteeing a reliable space transportation system for private business ventures.

But, as we shall see, NASA appears instead to be providing high-cost benefits to segments of the infant space industry while the space agency struggles to maintain a virtual monopoly of space transportation by discouraging lower-cost private competitors.

Two examples of the third category of federal services (supposedly common-pool goods) will also be considered. The air traffic control system was at the center of controversy during the first Reagan administration because of the PATCO strike. Flight control services are delivered by the federal government on the mistaken assumption that they are a collective good that the private sector could not supply. Yet federal provision leads to enormous hidden costs to the country, large benefits for certain individuals, and the misallocation of resources. The Department of Defense, on the other hand, suffers from problems similar to those of federal health-care programs. In providing collective protection to the nation, the Defense Department contracts out weapons production to the private sector. But unsound management and poor program design have turned contracting out from a device to improve efficiency into a vehicle that allows private firms to print money.

In each of these examples, a form of privatization would allow the stated purpose of the program to be achieved with far less drain on the Treasury. Moreover, the political task of encouraging privatization in these areas is likely to be a good deal easier than it is for, say, human-service programs. One important reason for this is that in instances such as the Postal Service and weapons production, the public-spending coalition has outstayed its welcome, and public opinion seems willing to support alternative methods of delivering the service. Another reason is that the elements of an effective privatization coalition often seem to be in place. Indeed, federal services appear to be an area of government where the political environment is particularly ready for the privatization technique.

The U.S. Postal Service

Why Service Is Costly and Inefficient

The U.S. Postal Service (USPS) is the nearest equivalent in the United States to a European nationalized industry. Although it does not have a complete monopoly, it does have the exclusive right to provide a key service: the delivery of first-class mail. And postal employees are in the happy position of knowing that whatever their level of job performance and productivity, they work for an organization that cannot go bankrupt and can always pass on its inflated costs to the consumer or the Treasury.

In the early days of the Republic, the Post Office and the federal bureaucracy were practically synonymous. The growth of the federal bureaucracy at the time was due almost entirely to the expansion of employment in the postal system. From 1816 to the Civil War, for instance, 86% of the eightfold increase in civilian federal employment resulted from the recruitment of additional postal workers.[1] The purpose of the government-owned postal system in the United States, as in other countries, was to promote commerce and the cohesion of the nation by providing a universal and standardized method of communication. The assumption was that the private sector could not or would not deliver such a comprehensive service.

This rosy view of the Post Office quickly began to fade, however. Political scientist James Q. Wilson writes that although the widely held belief that the nineteenth-century service became the domain of political placement is exaggerated, federal ownership did mean that the Postal Service steadily acquired the typical characteristics of a nationalized industry:

> By the mid-twentieth century, slow and inadequate service, an inability technologically to cope with the mounting flood of mail, and the inequities of its pricing system became all too evident. The problem with the Post Office, however, was not omnipotence but impotence. It was a government monopoly. Being a monopoly, it had little incentive to find that most efficient means to manage its service; being a government monopoly, it was not free to adopt such means even when found—communities, congressmen, and special-interest groups saw to that.[2]

As the British discovered after World War II, when they nationalized major segments of the economy, public-sector employees have a strong tendency to see the public interest as secondary to their own and to rely on their government-sanctioned monopoly status to protect their inefficiency. The U.S. Postal Service has been no exception to this general rule: Labor costs have risen while service has declined. A 1982 General Accounting Office report, for instance found that USPS janitors are paid more than double the rate for contracted personnel doing the same work, and that $90 million a year could be saved simply by using non-USPS janitors.[3] Postal workers are well paid for their efforts. The average annual salary for postal employees is now approximately $27,000 in salary and benefits.

The monopoly on first-class mail enables the Postal Service to pass on these costs to the customer. Despite price increases far in excess of the inflation rate, service levels have declined. Business deliveries have been cut back, office hours shortened, and home delivery eliminated for houses built since 1978. Yet there is nothing particularly surprising in this. To an economist it has all the hallmarks of classic monopoly: "Productivity" improvements are in fact achieved by service reduction, and inflated labor costs are financed by increasing prices to the consumer.

The true financial shape of the Postal Service is by no means easy to determine. Between 1971 and 1979, the USPS received an annual operating subsidy of $920 million from Congress. Congress intended for this subsidy to decline to $460 million a year in 1984 and stabilize at that level thereafter. The direct operating subsidy, however, has been ended. On the other hand, the picture is made complicated by a subsidy for special subsidized rates enjoyed by certain users, such as nonprofit organizations. For FY 1985, such "revenue forgone" was expected to amount to $800 million. Similarly the in-built subsidy to rural America and other high-cost users imposes considerable burdens on the Postal Service that should be taken into consideration. However, the right of USPS to borrow at below market rates, the assets it acquired free of charge during reorganization, and the unfunded liability of its pension plan are all subsidies that should be factored into the balance sheet of the $24-billion-a-year agency. The health coverage and pension plans available to postal workers alone have unfunded liabilities equivalent to $1 billion a year, according to the Congressional Budget Office. Yet these plans are not operated by the Postal Service, and so the shortfall does not appear in the USPS balance sheet.

Unlike many other federal services, however, the Postal Service must charge for its services. Were this not so, the USPS would no doubt be providing all manner of popular services below their actual cost, with the resulting deficit spread across all taxpayers. But as explained in Chapter 2, user charges do have the effect of bringing at least some notion of cost to service users, causing them to compare the level of service with that available from alternatives at similar prices.

Although the Private Express statutes prevent private-sector carriers from competing directly with the first-class letter market of the Postal Service, the user charge requirement on the USPS has opened up the opportunity for many private firms to bite at the heels of the nation's letter carriers. United Parcel Service, for instance, has captured over 80% of the parcel business from USPS. And a number of overnight and intracity courier services have cut into the commercial letter business. Companies have also emerged to cover gaps in USPS's own services. For instance, the Postal Service claims it can achieve great savings by delivering mail to a post office box rather than to the recipient's home. The only problem is that there is a chronic shortage of such boxes in many cities. So private box services have sprung up to cater to the demand. Another company, World Mail Center, plans to franchise a computerized system that offers a high-tech alternative to the labor-intensive post office counter and seemingly endless customer lines. The new centers will enable customers to route their mail through the most cost-effective means, with all the necessary paperwork taking an average of twenty-five seconds. The company's chairman calls the service a "travel agent for letters and packages."[4]

Like most monopolies, the Postal Service has no love for competition and uses the law whenever possible to stifle it. The USPS has moved swiftly, for instance, to stamp out the private delivery of Christmas cards by cub scouts and charity groups. And when it has developed new services, it has been keen to keep them all for itself. The Postal Service began to explore electronic mail in 1977, for example. Two years later, according to the Postal Rate Commission, which regulates USPS, the Service was busily examining ways to ban private competitors.[5] It did not manage to do so—and just as well, because its electronic service, E-COM, has been a disaster. Despite a $40 million investment, customer resistance caused E-COM to lose over a dollar on every letter it delivered.[6] Meanwhile, Federal Express's new electronic mail service, ZAP MAIL, has quickly overtaken E-COM—and has done so without the help of a subsidy.

Privatizing the Postal Service

It is impossible to assess fully the total subsidy to individuals, such as rural dwellers, inherent in the Postal Service monopoly, or the burden on the nation's economy arising from the Service's inefficiency. But moving the function out of the public sector entirely would bring competitive pressures to bear on the delivery of first-class mail, forcing greater efficiency and almost certainly a reduction in price.

Many free-market economists argue that the underlying inefficiency of the Postal Service monopoly over first-class mail can never be cured as long as the monopoly continues to exist.[7] If the monopoly were ended, of course, there would be enormous competitive pressure to bring prices in line with costs. If a legally regulated uniform price were maintained throughout the industry, defenders of the monopoly argue, private companies would simply move into the high-density urban markets, leaving the Postal Service with loss-making rural routes—but without the ability to cross-subsidize. And if there were no price regulation, they maintain, prices in urban areas would fall rapidly, while rural dwellers would have to pay heavily for even the most basic services.

Strict free marketeers respond that higher postal costs should just be one cost to weigh against the benefits of living in the countryside. Subsidizing postal service to rural areas, they point out, merely distorts choices in favor of living outside large metropolitan areas, and this is a costly and pointless exercise when subsidies are also given to draw people into the city (such as federal support for mass transit). So ending the postal monopoly and uniform pricing would be just one step toward ending the current maze of contradictory subsidies.

Could the postal monopoly be ended? Widespread public irritation with the Postal Service might eventually break down the natural tendency of most people to stick with the "simplicity" of a uniform price structure. On the other hand, there are more urban dwellers and businesses likely to gain from price competition than there are rural firms and residents who might lose by it. So a strong privatization coalition might well rally around a proposal to end the monopoly. But even if rural opposition did prove to be too strong, much can be said for buying out the rural constituency.

James Bovard calculates that the annual subsidy to rural delivery amounts to about $600 million. He notes also that Postal Rate Commissioner John Crutcher has estimated that inflated federal employee wages alone may add as much as $3 billion to USPS costs. Since the high cost of mail delivery stems from these excessive labor costs, not rural delivery as such, Bovard maintains that it would be less expensive for the country if Congress simply appropriated $600 million to subsidize rural delivery instead of maintaining an inefficient service covering the whole country.[8] But a special federal levy on all first-class mail carried by private firms, with the revenue used to subsidize deliveries to rural areas, might be preferable to an appropriation. A levy would keep the cross-subsidy within the industry. And because the subsidy costs would thus be concentrated on certain delivery firms and their customers, not the general taxpayer, strong and well-organized lobbying pressure could be counted on to keep the subsidy low.

Short of such complete privatization, contracting out would be a method of moving toward a postal system sensitive to market pressures, while maintaining a role for the federal government as the facilitator, but not the provider, of first-class mail delivery. In this instance the government would still be responsible for maintaining the principle of uniform service and price, but private contractors would be invited to bid for the right to supply rural segments of the service. This is clearly a second-best solution from an economist's viewpoint. But it would be less radical, and probably more feasible politically, than outright privatization.

Contracting out would not be new for the Postal Service. Nearly all intercity mail transportation is already contracted out to private firms. And almost 5,000 delivery routes have been signed over to private carriers, saving up to two-thirds of normal costs.[9] In addition, the Postal Service has consolidated many of its local offices into community post offices operated by private contractors. The General Accounting Office estimated in 1981 that between $125 million and $150 million could be saved annually if 7,000 limited-service offices were to be replaced by such community offices or by extended rural routes.[10]

Within the context of a federal postal system, contracting out could provide new services to customers. Private contractors could be used to enhance a basic service provided by the Postal Service. As home delivery gradually disappears, for instance, residents could be permitted to contract with private home-delivery companies, which would transport mail from the local post office to its final destination—perhaps private companies could "piggyback" such a service with the regular delivery of newspapers.

Postal Rate Commissioner Crutcher suggests that the entire rural service should be put out for private bidders as each route becomes vacant. He believes this should be the first step toward privatizing large segments of the Postal Service. Crutcher estimates that the country could save 25% of the current $24 billion annual budget of the USPS by adopting his plan. "Ultimately," says the commissioner, "my proposal would introduce competition to the Postal Service by privatizing the processing, delivery, and retail functions in each city and awarding them periodically as franchises to the lowest bidder."[11]

Contracting out the Postal Service in this way would enable the system to be moved gradually into the private sector. Given the inefficiency of the current service and the low regard in which it is held by the public, it is likely that the coalition wishing to retain the system entirely within the public sector (a coalition consisting chiefly of postal employees) would be no match for a privatization coalition of private carrying companies and their potential customers. Eventually, the federal role could shrink to that of a regulator, with its subsidy limited to support for high-cost routes.

Commercial Space Transportation

Supporters of NASA are fond of pointing out favorable comparisons between the space agency and the Postal Service. They argue that NASA, like the USPS, is a federally funded agency pursuing a public purpose that the private sector cannot serve. And they also maintain that just as the Postal Service stimulated the growth of commercial airlines in the 1920s by guaranteeing them critical business, so NASA is now stimulating the development of a commercial space industry, both by undertaking expensive long range research and by providing the infant industry with a sophisticated and efficient transportation system.

It is not unreasonable to claim that certain NASA operations fulfill a public purpose. Assuming that government has a duty to facilitate primary research, NASA's deep space exploration can be justified, as could the uplifting national quest to put an American on the moon. Similarly, the defense aspects of space science are an important part of the federal government's principal purpose of defending the nation. But the contention that the federal government should undertake commercially related operations is quite another matter.

NASA justifies the shuttle-based National Space Transportation System (NSTS) in the same manner that government energy officials tried to justify projects such as the Clinch River Breeder Reactor and the Synthetic Fuels Corporation—by claiming that it is a basically commercial project that is simply too expensive and long-grange for the private sector to undertake. But just as Clinch River and Synfuels led to the expenditure of enormous amounts of taxpayer resources without regard to market conditions (but to the benefit of firms favored with government contracts), the shuttle program is quickly becoming a very expensive way of saving a few private firms some development costs. Moreover, just as the Postal Service vigorously defends its monopoly from potential competition, so NASA is trying to corner the space transportation market and make life difficult for its more entrepreneurial competitors. Only by privatizing the NSTS and requiring private firms to pay the full cost of the private commercial benefits they receive will the nation avoid the prospect of a space-transportation monopoly operated with the inefficiency of the Postal Service.

The entrance of NASA into the business of space transportation is an interesting example of how federal agencies seek to expand their scope in order to stay in existence, and thereby provide employment to their workers and private-sector contractors. The space agency has conducted a masterly public-relations campaign to ensure its continued survival—aided, of course, by aerospace firms with millions of dollars in projects on the line. The original scope of NASA was confined to research and demonstration projects, but once the Apollo program began to run down, NASA officials began to push strongly for the agency to be given the job of overseeing commercial space transportation. The agency was very successful in winning support for this change of role, and thanks to the shuttle it now seems well entrenched in the commercial space industry.

The shuttle program, however, shows just what can happen when a federal agency is allowed to venture into what is more properly a private commercial field. The shuttle was designed by scientists, not businessmen, and it reflects the interests of its designers. It may be a valuable vehicle for defense and specialized research, but when it comes to standard commercial tasks such as satellite launches, the shuttle is a state-of-the-art Cadillac trying to do the job of a pickup truck. In the bottom-line world of the emerging space industry, the costly delays and malfunctions associated with the shuttle have begun to mean serious problems for the private customers it was supposed to assist.

One of the arguments used to support the $4-billion-a-year NSTS budget was that a federally financed space transportation service was needed to get the commercial space industry literally off the ground. Yet the private sector has not been slow to develop alternative transportation systems. A number of private firms, for instance, pressed the federal government to make launch facilities available for private launches using surplus federal unmanned rockets, and the Reagan administration announced in 1984 that it would reduce barriers to such ventures. And a small but expanding number of space entrepreneurs have even begun experimenting with completely private launch systems.

Just as the Postal Service has often made it clear that competition is unwelcome, the federal government has in the past placed many obstacles in the path of these private space-transportation companies. One barrier has been federal regulation. Until the Reagan administration began to reduce the paperwork, space entrepreneurs planning a launch had to obtain approvals from up to seventeen different agencies, ranging from the Department of State to the Bureau of Alcohol, Tobacco and Firearms. One company experimenting with sea-based launches even had to apply for a special export license.

Red tape is a costly irritant that can be reduced, given enough private pressure and an administration committed to simplifying regulation. A much greater barrier, paradoxically, results from

NASA's policy of underpricing its services in order to attract private customers. According to an examination of shuttle pricing policies by Milton Copulos, NASA's typical $20-million price tag for a satellite launch is less than one-fourth of the true cost; the rest is picked up by the taxpayer. The true cost of private rocket launches is much less than that of the shuttle—about $25 million to $30 million—but private firms must cover their full costs and charge accordingly.[12] The result: the shuttle can undercut its far less costly private competitors. And although NASA delivers a service that in theory the private sector cannot provide, the agency is actually engaged in an aggressive marketing campaign to beat out foreign and private competitors.

The argument for a taxpayer-funded space-transportation system rests on the assumption that despite the potential commercial gains from a space industry, the private sector somehow lacks the resources to realize that potential—or is unwilling to take the necessary risks. But this argument is seriously flawed. When private industry refuses to invest in new ventures, it does so not because it lacks the funds or the vision of government officials, but because the probable future rewards do not justify the resources that must be used. When the potential profit is worth the risk, the private sector has always been willing to invest enormous amounts of money. A dry hole in the North Sea means the loss of millions of dollars to an oil company, but when drilling rights were auctioned in the 1960s and 1970s, private companies poured billions of dollars into those treacherous waters in search of oil.

Private companies are clearly beginning to see the chance of significant profits from space. Commercial satellites are already a highly lucrative business, and the emergence of limited-service private launch companies demonstrates the keen interest of private firms in space transportation. Factories in space may also open up new major markets. Johnson & Johnson and McDonnell Douglas, for instance, expect $1 billion in annual sales from just the first of up to ten new medicines they intend to process in space.[13] Many other firms are just as optimistic. Yet the private space industry, and particularly private transportation companies, in the long run may be hindered by the "helping hand" of NASA. Private companies are usually quite happy to see the taxpayers picking up part of their costs, and so they are very willing to patronize a subsidized shuttle rather than a higher-priced (but actually less costly) private alternative. There is no shortage of venture capital, most investment experts agree, but few investors are keen to put up money when it might be donated instead by government. According to James Connor, managing director of the First Boston Corporation, private funding would flow far more rapidly if the government would just keep out of the picture: "As long as it appears that the government is going to be able to do it, or is willing to do it, you won't find real demand for private space services. And there will be no significant space commercialization on the launching side until people think the space shuttle won't take care of their needs for the foreseeable future."[14]

The demand for federal spending on space services that benefit private companies will continue to increase as long as government is willing to price those services below cost—and below the price that private launch firms can reasonably charge. There is no reason why certain private companies should be subsidized in this way, just because their profits come from space. And there is good reason to move the space-transportation function back into the private sector where it belongs before NASA becomes a costly Amtrak in space.

The privatization of the NSTS would present few technical problems, but interest-group politics would make the process difficult. The public generally has a romanticized view of the space agency, so there is no groundswell of taxpayer anger demanding a reduction in NASA's budget. Moreover, as long as the shuttle is reliable—which is perhaps becoming more doubtful—private users of the orbiter have an incentive to continue supporting the taxpayer-subsidized system.

But private launch companies may be acquiring more muscle. Delays and failures in the shuttle program are causing launch business to be lost to foreign systems using expendable rockets, in particular the French Ariane system and the Japanese. This loss of business overseas may prove to be enough to tip the scales of public opinion toward more reliance on a simpler private launch system. Support for privatization may also harden as the enormous potential of the space industry becomes clearer and people begin to ask why such profitable ventures need subsidies from Uncle Sam.

If the administration wishes to hasten the creation of a privatization coalition, it should press forward on three fronts. In the first place, it should accelerate the policy announced in 1984 of making existing ground-launch facilities and space technology more available to private launch companies. At the same time it should begin to raise shuttle prices to reflect the full cost of the system. It should also sell the shuttles that are not required for military purposes. There are already strong indications that the existing shuttles could be sold, bringing a healthy flow of cash into the Treasury. Astrotech International Corporation, wishing to become the commercial operator of the space-transportation system, has already offered $1.5 billion for an existing shuttle and a further $2 billion for a new shuttle.[15]

The willingness of private companies to enter high-risk and costly ventures demonstrates the spuriousness of the argument that government money is necessary to develop technologies supposedly beyond the means or vision of private enterprise. Federally financed space transportation is but one of many "unmet needs" that government officials have identified, leading to federal programs that benefit private industry while imposing costs on the taxpayer. The $8.8-billion Clinch River Breeder Reactor, for instance, was supposed to address the "crisis" of escalating uranium prices with a new but expensive technology—but the price of uranium fell, making the project uneconomical. Even so, local political and industry pressure almost managed to keep the project alive. It was defeated only when an unholy alliance of Naderite environmentalists and fiscal conservatives eventually managed to block funding in Congress, after $2 billion had already been spent.[16] Similarly, the "farsighted" Energy Department sought to correct a "market failure" in the development of new energy sources, this time on the assumption that oil prices would skyrocket, by successfully urging Congress in 1980 to create the $20 billion Synthetic Fuels Corporation to subsidize the development of new fuels. But the price of oil did not skyrocket, and by 1984 the corporation found itself guaranteeing some projects to the tune of $92 a barrel of synthetic oil—about three times the cost of natural oil.

The successes and failures of campaigns to defeat costly subsidies to industry provide some useful lessons for tactics to privatize federal services. It appears, for instance, that such federal subsidies to industry usually can be stopped only when a rival coalition, believing itself to be hurt by a program, is able to out-lobby the public spending coalition. Fiascos such as Synfuels may create sufficient public outrage to end the subsidy. Stopping costly and uneconomic demonstration projects, such as Clinch River, may unfortunately depend mainly on lobbying by anti-business groups. Federal projects to help certain players in potentially profitable ventures such as space, on the other hand, may fall victim to privatization coalitions based on interest groups that are being pushed out of the marketplace by the project. What an administration has to do to aid this process is to take steps to strengthen the privatization coalition, so that it can mount a political challenge against those who benefit from the taxpayer.

The Air Traffic Control System

Although NASA's role in space commercialization is based on the myth that a gap exists in the private marketplace, the government provides other services on the argument that they are toll or collective goods which must be consumed jointly. An interesting example of such a federal service, in view of the controversies surrounding it in recent years, is the nation's air traffic control (ATC) system. Despite the routine delays, the 1981 strike, low morale, and other problems associated with the federally operated system, most air travelers assume that controlling the airways is a service that only governments can provide. The system is a natural monopoly that all aircraft must utilize for safe travel, many believe, and there seems to be a consensus that the profit-making, corner-cutting private sector cannot be entrusted with safety in the air.

The $4-billion-a-year ATC program is administered through the Department of Transportation and financed by a system of airport and ticket taxes. It provides traffic flow services between airports and operates control towers at all major and most minor airports. The controllers are employees of the federal government.

The federally owned monopoly is plagued with problems, however. According to Robert Poole and others, these difficulties stem inevitably from the fact that the government operates the system. The ATC system, he says, suffers from the same deficiencies as any other federal bureaucracy: "Lack of competition removes strong incentives for economic efficiency. Obtaining revenue via taxation precludes the direct feedback from users inherent in buyer-seller relationships in the marketplace. Civil service regulations significantly restrict the efficient use of personnel. And political control makes long-range planning difficult."[17] Shifting the function into the private sector, Poole argues, would end the structural problems, reduce system costs, and eliminate many of the hidden but considerable indirect costs imposed on the economy by delays and misallocation.[18]

According to Poole, the shortcomings of the federally run system reflect its sensitivity to political pressures rather than to market signals. The 250,000 small aircraft users, for instance, have managed to block the installation of effective collision-avoidance systems that would in turn mean restrictions on private aircraft. They have also prevented the implementation of a market-based system of user fees that would reduce congestion by placing higher charges on private planes wishing to land at peak times. Government ownership, says Poole, is also at the root of the poor working conditions and labor relations in the system. Although the Professional Air Traffic Controllers Organization (PATCO) seriously underestimated the determination of Ronald Reagan in 1981, union militants had generally been able to exploit their monopoly position. And rigid bureaucratic management in the system has only added fuel to the labor relations fire.

The public's tolerance of the inadequate and costly system, says Poole, arises from its acceptance of the myth that the system is a natural monopoly that can be operated only by government. But ATC is not a monolithic system, he notes. Tower controllers feed into regional and national networks, and there is no need for individual airports to be operated by federal employees just because they feed into a unified network—any more than AT&T or other long-distance telephone companies have to own local telephone companies or the equipment installed in a home. All that is needed is compatibility of procedures. In fact, when the government withdrew services from many small (so-called Level I) airports after the PATCO strike in order to strengthen services at the larger airports, a number of these airports contracted out services to private firms. The savings have been remarkable. Typically the bill for a private service is one-third to one-half the cost for federal controllers. Farmington, New Mexico, for example, now pays $90,000 for private control service by FAA-certified controllers, while the government spent nearly $300,000 a year to staff the same tower.[19]

Privately operated airport towers do not cost less because controllers are inadequately trained or the facilities are ill-equipped. The private controllers are usually retired, and very experienced, former federal controllers. But instead of the "cost is no object" government attitude to equipment and the rigid work rules that characterize a government bureaucracy, private control centers use functional equipment and flexible work rules. There are currently 283 Level I and Level II (that is, small) towers. If all these were contracted out, says Poole, their 2,316 experienced controllers could be moved to busier facilities and considerable savings achieved.[20] Who would provide private services at smaller airports? In addition to retired controllers, probably many of the 11,500 controllers fired from their jobs in 1981. Larry Phillips, national secretary for the U.S. Air Traffic Controllers Organization, formed from the ashes of PATCO, strongly supports such privatization. He notes that the management responsibilities routinely undertaken by controllers in small towers tend to "enrich the work experience and improve overall morale and performance," in contrast to the "rigid, bureaucratic" conditions in federally operated towers.[21]

Phillips also supports Poole's suggestion for more extensive privatization. Poole explains that far from the private sector being unable to provide national ATC services, private systems are already in existence in countries such as Switzerland and Saudi Arabia. He argues that a system operated by the private sector would be safe—since it would always be under the threat of expensive lawsuits if there was negligence—while competition would ensure efficiency.

Such a system would charge full user fees for all its services, and consist of two levels:

> The top level would be an ATC system corporation with overall system design and coordination responsibility. The System Corporation would contract out the operation of individual en route and approach/departure control centers to ATC Operating Companies. The Operating Companies would be profit-making firms, perhaps including the existing U.S. control tower contractors and such aerospace firms as Bendix and Lockheed. The ATC System Corporation would be a not-for-profit firm ... with user organizations as stockholders.[22]

This two-level private system, says Poole, would ensure complete independence from politics. The national nonprofit corporation would be owned by airlines and other users. They would have every incentive to maintain safety and to introduce technical and work-rule innovations to improve efficiency and reduce costly delays to the users. And by contracting out local services through competitive franchises, the corporation could avoid monopolistic union or owner practices.

The prospects for privatization of the ATC system are surprisingly good. User fees are now charged to airlines and passengers through special taxes—even though they are inequitable. So, like those of the first-class mail system, the costs are mainly concentrated on the users, not spread thinly across all taxpayers. Consequently these users have a pecuniary interest in cost reduction. Moreover, given the growing morale problems among federal air traffic controllers, it is unlikely that they would be implacable opponents of change. Meanwhile, many of the controllers fired in 1981 are eager to return to work. By dealing with them as contractors rather than employees, the government would not have to back down on its 1981 decision to exclude the strikers from federal jobs.

The complete privatization suggested by Poole, he admits, is still too radical to be adopted as a single package. Even when the public is persuaded by the logic of a major change, usually it still wants to go forward gradually, especially where safety is concerned. People would have to feel very safe in privatized segments of the sky before entrusting their lives to a national private system. The most sensible approach, therefore, might be to introduce the system slowly, so that a coalition of supporters can develop and grow. Initially, the administration could begin to contract out control functions at the smaller airports. This would be popular with overworked controllers and former PATCO members. Local airport support for such a move would be stimulated if Washington agreed to share some of the cost savings with the airports, thereby giving them a financial incentive to back privatization.

The next step, suggests Larry Phillips, would consist of "taking a major tower out of the system as an experimental enterprise zone and letting it be run by a consortium of airlines."[23] Poole suggests that a major en route control center should also be put out to bid: "A geographically isolated region such as south Florida would make an excellent test area for such privatization."[24] By moving forward in this incrementalist way, creeping privatization could win increasing support. Eventually it would lead to the removal of federal employees and bureaucratic inefficiencies from the nation's control towers, saving air travelers millions of dollars every year.

Defense Spending

The most significant and expensive federal service of all, of course, is defense. FY 1985's defense budget was expected to consume $266 billion of the nation's resources, accounting for 27% of the entire federal budget. Unlike the other federal services discussed in this chapter, defense can truly be called a collective good: It has to be "consumed" jointly by all citizens, and assigning user charges to individual "consumers" would be impossible. Moreover, there is almost complete agreement that national defense is a responsibility of the federal government. Overall planning and funding for defense cannot be delegated to the states (except for minor elements, such as local reserves or civil defense), and certainly not to the private sector.

As noted in Chapter 2, however, there is still no reason in principle why a national government's responsibility to guarantee provision of a good or service must mean that the government itself should actually make the good or provide the service—and there are good efficiency and political reasons why it should not. As with many other collective goods, contracting out this function to private-sector suppliers can lead to significant savings. But it was also pointed out in Chapter 2 that contracting out has dangers as a form of privatization. Private suppliers of government services have strong incentives to lobby for increased spending levels, to try to monopolize the service in order to push up costs (a major problem as we saw, in the provision of human services), and to arrange sweetheart contracts with government departments. For contracting out to be efficient, it was noted, strong and open competition must characterize the contract process.

Approximately 25% of the defense budget—overwhelmingly weapons procurement—is contracted out to private-sector firms. To put it mildly, weapons procurement has not been a good advertisement for this method of privatization. Almost daily media stories of multibillion-dollar cost overruns, outrageous prices charged for standard spare parts, and disturbing lobbying practices have made many people wonder if the defense industry can ever be expected to deliver a quality product at a reasonable price. But contracting out can be only as good as the bureaucracy that designs the contract requirements and evaluates the performance of the contractors. If a government agency has an excessively close relationship with the contractor, or if it bends under pressure to limit competition, then the profit motive that encourages efficiency in a competitive marketplace will lead instead to bloated costs and profiteering. Only by reforming the contract procedures and reintroducing real competition will the benefits of contracting out be realized.

The underlying reason why expenditures on weapons systems are out of hand is that a public spending coalition drives the process, just as it perpetuates other federal programs. Contractors and government officials have many incentives to lobby for increased spending and to support costly overruns. Expensive weapons systems mean jobs. And as the watchdog Project on Military Procurement points out, for all the talk in Congress about controlling military spending and for all the righteous indignation about overruns, legislators have good reasons to talk one way but vote another:

> Congressmen with major defense contractors or bases in their districts have always welcomed the benefits of immense, unstoppable programs in their districts. And many more Congressmen are being drawn in as the contractors and the procurement bureaucracy become increasingly expert at the very expensive practice of insuring against cancellation by spreading contracts for each juggernaut procurement to at least 48 of the 50 states.[25]

Even more disturbing, however, is the cozy symbiotic relationship that has developed between the contracting companies and the Pentagon bureaucracy. As in other areas of the government, the compatibility of interest of weapons producers and government officials explains much of the growth in spending and a good deal of the powerful resistance mounted against efforts to reform the process. According to Murray Weidenbaum, formerly President Reagan's top economic adviser, the scale of defense contracting and the dependency of huge private companies on those contracts make many of these companies more like branches of the government than like traditional entrepreneurs: "In a sense, the close, continuing relationship between the Department of Defense and its major suppliers is resulting in the convergence between the two which is blurring and reducing much of the distinction between public and private activities in an important branch of the American economy."[26]

As James Q. Wilson points out, however, the inherent cost problems of the Pentagon cannot really be attributed to the shadowy machinations of some military-industrial complex that is immune to democratic control. In fact, he reminds us, military outlays contain the greatest degree of discretionary spending in the entire federal budget. The problems can more logically be attributed to the fact that while Pentagon officials may wear uniforms, they are nonetheless bureaucrats. And the bureaucratic system within which they operate has serious deficiencies that lead inevitably to enormous waste and misallocation:

> The bureaucratic problems associated with the military establishment arise mostly from its internal management and are functions of its complexity, the uncertainty surrounding its future deployment conflicts, its constituent services over mission and role, and the need to purchase expensive equipment without the benefits of a market economy that can continue costs. Complexity, uncertainty, rivalry, and monopsony are inherent (and frustrating) aspects of the military as a bureaucracy.[27]

These bureaucratic deficiencies have resulted in serious impediments to efficient contracting. These barriers must be removed if the momentum enjoyed by the defense spending lobby is to be ended and if the nation is to achieve the goal of effective defense at a reasonable cost.

Two of the Pentagon's responsibilities have been especially distorted by bureaucratic shortcomings and by the incestuous relationship between government officials and private contractors. These are the procedures for competitive bidding and the testing function. Each is key to decisions regarding which weapons systems will be manufactured and what the final cost of the chosen systems will be.

The general issue of competitive bidding, however, must be examined according to the type of contract in question. Although only 6% of defense contracts are awarded by fully competitive bidding, it is obvious that there is a very big difference between trying to solicit a wide range of bids on a highly specialized, expensive new secret missile, and buying standard typewriters for the Pentagon typing pool. As noted in Chapter 2, the Department of Defense administers the federal government's largest A-76 program—the program that requires departments to conduct cost comparisons between in-house and private-sector suppliers of standard commercial goods and services. But while the Office of Management and Budget study of the years 1980–82 found that savings from the program averaged 27% for each contract, A-76 covered only 235 contracts, saving about $250 million—an insignificant fraction of the total Pentagon budget.[28] Even this, angry private contractors charge, has been fiercely resisted and distorted by the Pentagon bureaucracy and the public-sector unions. The cost-comparison procedures heavily favor in-house supplies, for instance, and union pressure has kept many functions off limits to private firms, on the doubtful argument that they involve sensitive national-security considerations.

Weapons development and procurement, on the other hand, is contracted out to private-sector firms. But the degree of competition is often limited or nonexistent. One reason for this, of course, is that ordering new front-line fighter aircraft is not like ordering paper clips. The cost of the technology is uncertain and there is no real market for making price comparisons or cost estimates. The need for secrecy and detailed specifications may also limit the possible suppliers to just one firm. Moreover, the scale and lead time involved in new systems can make it impossible for the Pentagon to switch suppliers or to cancel a program once it is under way.

These special characteristics of weapons procurement mean that the Defense Department should have a highly sophisticated testing and decision-making process and that it should maintain a careful separation between officials who test weapons systems and those who promote particular designs. But as procurement analyst Dina Rasor points out, many weapons systems manage to proceed through the development and production process because testing in the Pentagon is not independent of the research-and-development function. And since officials who have researched a system and urged its production are not inclined to admit that they have been guilty of poor judgment, there is a built-in tendency for defects found in testing to be discounted, and for expensive modifications to be preferred over cancellation.[29] This can lead to staggering cost overruns, she notes, and to sophisticated weapons that excite scientists but break down disastrously on the battlefield.

Most occupants of the White House have been fully aware of the problems associated with this mingling of the Pentagon's testing and procurement functions. President Eisenhower's experiences in World War II made him acutely aware of the need for a clear division of responsibility. As he noted in an important memorandum on the subject, written in 1946, "Within the army we must separate responsibility for research and development from the functions of procurement, purchase, storage and distribution."[30] The problem persisted, however, thanks in part to Pentagon foot-dragging and in part to the rapid defense build-up during the Vietnam War. Weapons failures in Vietnam, however, did contribute to the formation, in 1970, of a presidential panel to investigate weapons development.

The Nixon panel recommended the establishment of an independent Operational Testing and Evaluation group under civilian leadership and a separate, independent Defense Test Agency. Yet when the testing group was established, it reported to the director of defense research and engineering, the official responsible for research and procurement. The Carter administration was no more successful in reforming the process. Carter's initial plan was to separate testing completely from research and evaluation. But says Rasor:

> The R&D community saw this attempt as a direct attack on their ability to move weapons through the system without criticism. The attempted "coup" only lasted a little over a year. . . . [The Pentagon] convinced [Defense Secretary] Harold Brown to limit the staff of the new OT&E organization to eight people instead of the recommended 22 and had it made impossible for the group to obtain a formal charter that would allow them to ensure adequate operational listing. . . . [I]n October 1978, the independent OT&E office asked to be disbanded (a remarkable occurrence in any bureaucracy) because of the impossibility of carrying out its function without an appropriate staff and charter.[31]

Reforming the Procurement Process

Despite the Reagan administration's stated policy of bringing tight management back into government and introducing more competition into defense contracting, the record has been mixed. Costly overruns still plague weapons contracting. But the administration has scored some successes. The $20-billion B-1 bomber program is ahead of schedule and below cost—thanks, says the U.S. Air Force, to savings achieved from multiyear procurement and new incentives for cost savings.[32] On the other hand, convincing evidence that effective competition has been introduced generally into the procurement process is still hard to find.

Significant savings and efficiency improvements will not be achieved in the Department of Defense, however, until fundamental changes are made in the way the Pentagon buys its weapons. These reforms must concentrate on improving testing procedures and bringing effective competition into choosing a contractor.

The first priority must be the creation of an independent operational testing office that reports directly to the secretary of defense and has access to all budgets and data concerned with operational testing. Splitting this function away from the research-and-development arm of the Pentagon would increase the chances of defective weapons being canceled, because testers would have had no responsibility for the original design specifications and development choices.

A second step to increase competition from *within* the bureaucracy, says the Project on Military Procurement, would be to encourage different services to compete for the chance to oversee the research and development of a new system: "Eliminating overlap typically leads to the chartering of bureaucratic monopolies, which gives away the Secretary of Defense's (and the Congress's) more important lever in managing the bureaucracy."[33]

Wider use of competitive procurement is also necessary to improve the process of choosing a contractor. Competition within the bureaucracy would help to achieve this by fostering different, competing specifications. It might also be helped by more independent testing, since this would probably tend to favor simpler, more sturdy technology (which could be manufactured by several contractors) over the state-of-the-art exotica favored by many Pentagon researchers. Multiyear procurement, on the other hand, could be a mixed blessing. Contractors point out that costs are bound to rise when the long-term demand for a weapon system is uncertain, because it is difficult to plan ahead, obtain quantity discounts from subcontractors, and make efficient investments in plant and machinery. However, long-term commitments do mean less competition after the first year. They also mean that a contracting firm and its voting workers may become an even more entrenched part of the spending coalition, such that termination of a contract after the initial multiyear agreement becomes a difficult political proposition.

What are the chances of basic reforms in the Pentagon's contracting procedures? Probably much better than they have been for some time. After broad initial support for the Reagan defense build-up, anger has been mounting in many conservative and business organizations at the inefficiency prevalent in the Defense Department.[34] This irritation has been fanned by the disclosures of waste contained in the Grace Commission reports and other analyses of military spending. In some instances, conservatives concerned with budget deficits and the growth of spending have even begun to join forces with traditional liberal critics of the Pentagon. And representatives of small businesses who feel shut out of defense contracting by the established large firms are adding their voices to the protests.

A third component of a coalition to reform the procurement process may prove to be the military itself. Soldiers who have to lay their lives on the line have little sympathy with a system that gives them helicopters that break down in the Iranian desert and rifles that jam in the Vietnamese jungles. This group of "beneficiaries" of effective weapons could even become the vanguard of a coalition to demand basic structural changes in the Pentagon bureaucracy, so that the potential benefits of competitive contracting out can finally be realized.

6

SOCIAL SECURITY

The growth of the Social Security system is an example of the public spending coalition at its most effective. The system was established as a remedy to a social crisis; later a powerful coalition formed around the program, leading to an incremental expansion. On occasion—most recently at the beginning of the first Reagan administration—a serious attempt has been made to deal with its structural defects and to control its costs. And on each of these occasions the coalition has managed to survive the confrontation with scarcely more than a few bruises, while usually delivering its adversaries a political bloody nose.

Advocates of reduced federal spending point out that it is difficult to see how the federal government can shrink without cutbacks in Social Security. In 1983, some 36 million Americans received benefits under the program. The total cost of Social Security to the federal government that year, including benefits, administration, and other costs, was no less than $208 billion—amounting to 28.6% of the entire federal budget and only a billion dollars less than the nation spent on defense. These same advocates of spending reductions, however, also tend to believe that the prospects for any significant dent in Social Security outlays are very dim. The program now appears to have such a strong constituency that it is beyond control. The best that can be achieved, many feel, is some moderation in the growth of benefits.

As we shall see, however, Social Security spending may well be an area of the federal budget that is quite susceptible to the privatization strategy. Close examination of the constituency behind it shows that it is far from homogeneous, and that there are methods by which elements of that coalition could be detached, or by which their enthusiasm for the program could at least be reduced. Moreover, it is also evident that the makings of a countervailing privatization constituency already exist, coalescing around the seeds of a more attractive private alternative to Social Security for most Americans—Individual Retirement Accounts. Momentum for the expansion of IRAs has been gathering since 1982, when they became generally available. This momentum is likely to intensify, even if it is not actively encouraged by Congress or the administration. But if government officials and congressional leaders were actively to assist the IRA coalition with small tax and regulatory incentives, that momentum could lead to the creation, in stages, of a comprehensive private alternative to Social Security, and to a new political environment in which significant Social Security outlay reductions would be possible.

The Growth of Social Security

The Social Security program was enacted in 1935 in accordance with the recommendations of the Committee on Economic Security, the cabinet level panel that planned President Roosevelt's social welfare reform proposals of 1934. The Social Security Act provided for a federally administered system of old age benefits for workers. The benefits were to commence in 1942, and were to be financed by a payroll tax on employers and employees. This tax was to commence at 1% per person in 1937, rising in stages to 3% by 1949. Significantly, Congress defeated an amendment to the act that would have exempted firms with government-approved private pension plans from mandatory inclusion in the system.

Like many significant pieces of legislation, Social Security was enacted in an atmosphere of crisis—the depression—which generated the sense of urgency and the groundswell of popular support needed for passage.[1] But once the legislation was enacted, Martha Derthick notes in an analysis of Social Security policymaking, a coalition began to form around it which ensured that the program would grow:

> Social insurance had a number of properties that made it extremely appealing, or at least more acceptable than any likely alternatives, to the public, to officeholders in both major parties, and to interest groups (business and labor) that typically were at odds. Three such properties were particularly relevant to politics. First, the program was intrinsically incremental, which meant that costs would start low and grow gradually. Second, it promised taxpayers specific

benefits in return for their taxes, which both eased their willingness to pay taxes and alleviated whatever stigma was attached to getting the benefits. Third, it contained many compromises and ambiguities that enabled diverse interests to coalesce in support of it.[2]

Derthick explains that when Social Security began, only part of the work force was covered and the number of beneficiaries was small in comparison with the number of taxpayers. Consequently the tax burden could be kept low and widely based, while the beneficiaries and potential beneficiaries could expect significant returns during their retirement. In addition, the structure of the program had the additional political advantage that with any extension of coverage to new groups of workers, there would be an additional infusion of revenue into the system, while the corresponding new liabilities would not have a significant impact until much later.[3] In short, the Social Security system of 1935 was practically an open invitation to the formation of pressure groups urging expansion.

An impressive coalition did indeed develop, and it has been responsible for major increases in the benefits available under the system. The program administrators within the Social Security Administration (SSA) have proved to be a key element of this coalition, aiding the process of expansion by incrementation. Studies and proposals developed within the SSA have been based on the assumption that federally sponsored social insurance is the preferred method of addressing many of the nation's underlying social problems. "The prevailing technique of policy analysis [within SSA]," writes Derthick, "was to identify a social problem, such as lack of health care, and to develop the arguments and methods for dealing with it through social insurance" (Derthick, p. 25). According to Derthick, SSA executives "were also aware of being part of a worldwide movement" for government-operated social insurance, "and believed that there was logic, even inevitability, in what they were trying to do" (Derthick, p. 27).

The SSA staff has had an enormous behind-the-scenes influence on the politics of Social Security expansion. They have provided the staff—and thus, in practice, the policy options—for practically every advisory council or official study group formed to examine Social Security. These "impartial" councils, generally composed of representatives from labor, business, and "the public," have had a natural tendency to favor the retention or further development of the basic Social Security system. The councils provided for the SSA, notes Derthick, a convenient vehicle for what Philip Selznick calls "co-option"—that is, "the process of absorbing new elements into the leadership or policy-determining structure of an organization as a means of averting threats to its stability or existence" (quoted in Derthick, p. 90).

A close working relationship also developed between the SSA staff and organized labor. The relationship did not arise immediately, because many unions were concerned that Social Security would undermine union-regulated private pension plans, which were an inducement for workers to unionize. But after assiduous courting by Social Security officials, and a shift in view by the AFL and the CIO, organized labor became the principal advocate of more comprehensive Social Security coverage. The labor movement also became an unofficial outlet for the views of SSA officials, and its lobbying power—both directly and later through the National Council of Senior Citizens, which it created—was critical to the success of the campaign to establish Medicare and other extensions of the basic system of 1935.

SSA staff and labor leaders worked with friendly congressmen and representatives of beneficiary and near-beneficiary groups to create the political climate for expanding the program. "Pursuing welfare ends that were valued primarily by liberal interests with a commitment to expanding the public sector,"explains Derthick, "they cast them nonetheless in conservative terms, calculated to appeal to a society that valued individual work and sacrifice" (Derthick, p. 207). Proponents of the system talked of "contributions," not taxes, and talked about Social Security in the same terms as they would use to discuss a private self-insurance system.

The coalition generated political momentum for expansion by identifying near beneficiaries to add to the core of original beneficiaries. Once the basic system was in place, proposals were offered to ease eligibility requirements, extend coverage to new categories of workers, increase the benefit to tax ratio, and cover new types of risk. The strategy eventually began to show solid results. Disability benefits, for instance, were added in 1956, in spite of opposition from the American Medical Association and various business groups. After that victory took the steam out of its opponents, the coalition went on over the next several years to secure incremental improvements in those disability benefits.

Once disability insurance had been achieved, the coalition turned to medical care as the next major addition to the program. Once again, SSA officials provided the groundwork for new legislation. Organized labor played its part by pushing the Medicare issue into national prominence, and in 1960 it gained a commitment from presidential candidate John Kennedy to press for enactment of a Medicare bill. Thereafter, the coalition could count on the active participation of the administration, and obtained passage of Medicare legislation in 1965.

After disability and hospital insurance was grafted onto the original Social Security system, the coalition turned to winning significant improvements in the benefit structure:

> Insofar as expansion was linked to rising wages, the tendency to expansion was built in. It derived from the actuary's practice of basing his long-range cost estimates on the assumption that earnings would remain level. When earnings rose—as invariably they did—an actuarial surplus was "discovered." The SSA thereupon proposed benefit increases or other expansions, and Congress enacted them if an election was impending—as invariably there was. Thus the program was geared to the economic and political systems in a way that guaranteed its growth, and guaranteed that growth would be linked at least partially to wage increases rather than price increases, which typically were smaller (Derthick, p. 348).

Major benefit increases followed in 1969, 1971, and 1972, generally with congressmen trying to outbid one another for the support of the Social Security coalition. Thereafter an automatic adjustment was enacted, tied to cost of living increases.

The Social Security Ratchet

The political power of the public spending coalition behind Social Security has been evident during each of the campaigns for program expansion. SSA officials, labor leaders, and advocacy organizations representing beneficiaries and near-beneficiaries consistently have been able to take the initiative and tilt the political balance in their favor. By spreading costs widely, and phasing in tax increases over several years, they could promise substantial and concentrated benefits to segments of the population with comparatively small tax burdens on the general population. In any event, those segments would eventually become eligible for those same benefits. Thus the underlying public-choice advantage has remained with the proponents of expansion. And whenever the actuarial analysis suggested that the system had a long-run surplus (as in 1969), politicians could win easy electoral gratitude by passing "costless" benefit increases. When the long run position of Social Security looked precarious (as in 1977), on the other hand, Congress has responded with tax increases, not significant benefit cuts. The coalition is now so broadly based and the beneficiaries constitute such a powerful voting bloc that few politicians dare to risk criticizing the system.

The immense political damage that the Social Security coalition is able to inflict on its adversaries was evident in Ronald Reagan's ill-fated attempt to deal with the 1980–1981 crisis in Social Security funding by reducing benefits. The Reagan proposals were hardly draconian, especially when compared with the major benefit increases obtained in the previous fifteen years. They included a three-month postponement of the cost-of-living adjustment, cuts in certain benefits to the disabled, and a reduction in annual benefits to those choosing to retire early. Yet the plan was immediately besieged by bitter, often hysterical attacks mounted by the supporters of Social Security. Not surprisingly, Democratic politicians were quick to use the issue as a stick to beat the administration. The chairman of the House Select Committee on Aging, Claude Pepper, for instance, grimly described the Reagan plan as "the most fundamental assault" ever on the Social Security system, and House Speaker Thomas O'Neill denounced the proposals as "despicable."

Had the criticism been confined to traditional partisan attacks, Reagan might still conceivably have managed to obtain congressional passage of some key elements of the cost-cutting plan, especially given his success in winning other tax and budget votes in 1981. But the Social Security coalition closed ranks to take the initiative away from the White House. A formal coalition of ninety-six organizations, representing nearly 40 million Americans, was quickly formed to defend the system against the proposed cuts. Chaired by Wilbur J. Cohen, secretary of Health, Education and Welfare in 1968–69, and entitled Save Our Security (SOS), the coalition's board boasted a number of former SSA chairmen and commissioners. Its affiliated organization represented a cross section of America's most powerful lobbying groups and key constituencies, including the American Association of Retired Persons, the American Federation of State, County and Municipal Employees, the American Jewish Committee, the NAACP, the National Council of Churches, the National Council of Senior Citizens, the National Gray Panthers, the National Farmers Union, the National Urban League, and the U.S. Catholic Conference.

SOS directed withering fire at the administration. Wilbur Cohen accused "Ronald Reagan and the New Right Republicans" of plotting to "dismantle" Social Security through "cruel" cuts in benefits. Accusing the White House of using a "shortrun" funding problem as a pretext for destroying the financial security of elderly Americans, SOS argued that the system was basically sound, and that permitting the Old Age and Survivors' Insurance Trust Fund to borrow "temporarily" from the other Social Security funds would solve any immediate shortfall in revenues. If any further money was needed, argued the group, then loans from general revenues should be used. Support from general taxation, of course, opened the prospect of spreading the cost of Social Security wider, thereby tilting the long-run political balance even further toward the public spending coalition.

Amid mounting public and congressional opposition to his proposals, Reagan tried to defuse the issue and control the political damage by withdrawing his plan and appointing a commission, chaired by Alan Greenspan, to examine methods of solving the financial problems of the system. The commission did not report until after the elections of 1982, and the Democrats made good use of the specter of a dismembered Social Security system during the campaign.

The compromise finally hammered out by the commission, and passed by Congress with the endorsement of a shell-shocked White House, basically used the traditional formula for dealing with financial difficulties in the system. Of $168 billion in new revenue and savings to be achieved over six years, only $40 billion came from basic benefit reductions—and that merely by postponing for six months the cost-of-living increase scheduled to go into effect in July, 1983. An additional $30 billion came from the taxation of benefits for higher-income beneficiaries, but the bulk of the shortfall was covered by increasing payroll taxes ($58 billion) and by extending coverage to government employees and employees of nonprofit organizations ($23 billion).

Although the package did run into opposition from certain government employee unions, it had the support of SOS and other key groups such as the National Association of Manufacturers. Once again, the Social Security coalition was successful in protecting the system from fundamental reform and from any significant reduction in outlays. It handed Ronald Reagan a stinging defeat, and it reached a compromise that only added to the long-term momentum for expansion, thanks to two critical components in the final legislation. First, by raising payroll taxes the compromise meant that the federal ratchet clicked forward two more notches— new revenues were added to the system to finance a higher level of spending, and new payroll taxes encouraged workers to begin demanding higher benefits in return for their higher "contributions." And second, the compromise forced more Americans into the system, adding more voters to the lobby for a more generous Social Security system.

The Need for Structural Reform

A critical feature of the success of the Social Security coalition has been that it has managed to ignore, silence, or ridicule expert analysts who have questioned the basic structure of the program. Yet the work of such analysts clearly shows that the system is inherently unsound. The need to reform the system and reduce its outlays arises not only from the general problem of runaway costs but also from the fundamental flaws that will undermine Social Security's ability to continue providing benefits.

Martha Derthick notes that one reason for the negligible impact of dispassionate professional analyses on Social Security policymaking is that professionals have shown remarkably little interest in the program, despite its economic significance. After a number of papers and studies in the 1930s, few major analyses appeared until the 1960s, when the program was well established and expanding rapidly.

When economists and actuaries did begin to note disturbing inconsistencies and vagueness in the program, politicians and program administrators were quick to put pragmatism before logic. When Milton Friedman had the audacity, for instance, to criticize the basis of Social Security and characterize it as "a triumph of imaginative packaging and Madison Avenue advertising," former HEW Secretary Wilbur Cohen denounced him as "only an economist" who did not understand that inconsistency is an essential element of the art of public policy (Derthick, p. 165).

More surprisingly, ardent defenders of Social Security have managed to withstand the criticisms of several of the program's own professional chief actuaries, the key staff who calculate risks and probabilities for the system. These officials have shared the characteristic of becoming increasingly concerned about the soundness of the system. The first chief actuary, Rulon Williamson, eventually concluded that the system was seriously out of balance. He was apparently squeezed out of the SSA in 1949 and succeeded by Robert Myers, who seemed to be more in tune with the pragmatism of the SSA staff. But Myers, too, began to worry that the "expansionist" policies of SSA officials would endanger the U.S. economy. Unable to change policy from within, Myers resigned from the SSA in 1970 to express his dissent more freely. Yet his departure was virtually ignored, and his efforts have had no discernible effect on policymaking.

The SSA's chief actuary from 1975 to 1978, Haeworth Robertson, expresses similar grave doubts about the system. He maintains that the public perception of Social Security as a social insurance program could hardly be further from the truth. There is virtually no relationship, says Robertson, between an individual's Social Security taxes and his or her benefit levels—or, for that matter, between taxes and benefits on a group basis. Massive inequities exist within the system, and the nation faces a hidden Social Security liability several times greater than the national debt. If today's young workers are to receive the benefits they have been led to expect, Robertson calculates that they could face eventual payroll tax rates (combined employer and employee portions) of between 40% and 50%.[4]

According to several studies by Peter Ferrara, the long-run financing problems of Social Security stem from an inherent contradiction in the design of the program. The trouble with Social Security, says Ferrara, is that it attempts to pursue both welfare and insurance objectives. These contradictory objectives result in a system that provides bad welfare and bad insurance, and the political tension between these objectives has led inevitably to unsound financing.[5]

Ferrara maintains that the 1983 "rescue" package did nothing to resolve this contradiction, and so the long-term—and probably also the short-term—financing problems will continue to plague the system. He points out, that even using the SSA's own economic assumptions, the future of Social Security looks precarious, yet there is every reason to believe these assumptions are extremely optimistic. According to these assumptions, for instance, the fertility rate will increase substantially and permanently (except for the baby boom in the 1950s and 1960s, the trend has been steadily downward for two hundred years), inflation and unemployment will stabilize over the next eighty years at 4% and 6%, respectively, and the rate of increase in life expectancy will slow down significantly.[6] If these assumptions prove to be as unrealistic as they seem, says Ferrara, the system will have to be completely restructured or it will collapse.

A Framework for Privatization

The Objectives of Privatization

Several plans have been put forward to resolve the structural contradictions and financing problems of Social Security through privatization. These privatization plans generally involve two broad and concurrent steps based on privatization techniques for a service that is a private good, according to our classification in Chapter 2 (since retirement annuities and insurance protection are "consumed" by individuals, not by groups, and charges for the service can be applied to each individual).

The first step would be to split the program into two distinct parts: a welfare element and a social-insurance element. The welfare element would be tailored to provide support for low-income people, and it would be financed, like other welfare programs, from general taxation. The social-insurance element would be structured and financed according to normal actuarial principles, with payroll-related contributions and benefits strictly related to those contributions. By separating the elements in this way, proponents argue, the financing mythology would be ended once and for all, and the system's two elements could be financed on far sounder and fairer principles. Moreover, they argue, the complex intergroup transfers of income that characterize the politics of Social Security could then be disentangled, thereby weakening the momentum for continuous expansion of the system.

The second step in such plans concerns only the social-insurance element. If an insurance program is to be administered according to normal private-sector accounting principles, the argument goes, then there is no particular reason why that program should be operated by the federal government, and every political reason why it should not. This pure insurance element would be transferred to the private sector. Some privatizers would make such private social insurance strictly voluntary, but most would make it mandatory.

A privatization approach seems to offer the best prospect for a political and financial solution to runaway Social Security spending. By splitting the system into two clearly distinguishable elements, this approach would also divide the coalition, thereby allowing the policymaker to redesign the program in a manner that meets the requirements of each constituency, while offering to a key segment of the current Social Security coalition a private alternative that is more attractive than the existing federally operated system. In so doing, privatization could divert into the private sector a significant part of the demand for federal spending. In short, it could accomplish the twin goals of demand-side budget cutting: reducing federal spending while improving the quality of service to the public.

The Family Security Plan

The most realistic and carefully crafted model for a privatized Social Security system is that prepared by Peter Ferrara.[7] Under

Ferrara's family security plan, the welfare elements of the current Social Security system would be separated out and provided instead through the existing Supplemental Security Income (SSI) program. SSI is a means-tested, general-revenue financed program that provides income assistance to the elderly and disabled poor. By concentrating the income-support function of Social Security within a means-tested program financed by the general taxpayer, argues Ferrara, the government could assure low-income Americans with a solidly funded safety net for their retirement years.

The pure insurance functions of Social Security, according to the Ferrara plan, could be performed by an expanded version of Individual Retirement Accounts (IRAs). "Individuals would be allowed to purchase life, disability and old age health insurance through their IRAs so that their accounts would provide all the insurance benefits currently provided by Social Security."[8] He sees these expanded IRAs, or "Super IRAs," as an alternative to Social Security.

Unlike the current IRAs, which are deductible from taxable income, the new IRA contributions would be credited, dollar for dollar, against Social Security payroll taxes. Alternatively, says Ferrara, the IRA contributions could be credited against income taxes. The latter approach would mean that the flow of payroll-tax revenue into the Social Security system would be unaffected by workers choosing the IRA option. Each worker, in other words, would be required to contribute into a retirement program an amount equal to his or her payroll tax, but that worker would have the right to select between a private plan and the federal Social Security plan. The worker's future Social Security benefits, however, would be reduced according to the proportion of lifetime contributions the worker placed in the IRA option instead of in Social Security.

Ferrara pays close attention to the phasing in of his plan. If every worker in America were suddenly to opt out of Social Security in favor of an IRA, and if credits were taken against payroll tax rather than income tax, then clearly the system would collapse immediately, since there would be no income to cover Social Security's monthly checks. To avoid this, Ferrara proposes a gradual phase-in. Commencing in 1986, workers would be able to contribute up to 20% of their OASDHI[9] Social Security payroll taxes (plus the same proportion of their employer's share) to an IRA, modified to allow the purchase of hospital, disability, and term life insurance. This maximum credit would increase to 40% in 1996, to 66% in 2004, and to 100% in 2014. At each stage, the worker's Social Security benefit entitlement would be reduced in proportion to the credits applied to an IRA.

Ferrara accepts that a temporary shortfall of income over outlays would be inescapable during this phase-in period, since the revenue reductions would precede the reduction in the system's liabilities. To cover this period, he argues that privatizers must either bite the bullet and use general revenues to cover obligations to existing beneficiaries, or permit credits against income taxes. Ferrara calculates that the net shortfall to be covered would amount to $40 billion (in 1982 dollars) if the phase-in began in 1986. This figure would fall steadily to $4 billion by 1995, as savings in outlays began to be felt. When the second stage was implemented in 1996, the net cost would climb to $37 billion, falling to a net saving of more than $6 billion in 2003. The need for any support would cease in 2012, twenty-six years after the phase-in commenced. Thereafter, there would be a steady decline in the outlays of the Social Security system, as the private sector supplied an increasing proportion of total retirement benefits.[10]

Aside from achieving the objective of moving a major function of government into the private sector, Ferrara notes that privatizing Social Security in this way would have many advantages for beneficiaries and workers and thus would be very attractive to the public. The return on contributions invested, for instance, would likely be far better than it is under Social Security. Using the SSA's own assumptions, which he believes are very optimistic, Ferrara calculates that today's young workers face a real return on their Social Security contributions of less than 1% and possibly below 0% for two-career families. By contrast, several studies indicate that the real rate of return on equity investments has averaged 6% over the last 50 years.[11]

The IRA alternative would be even more beneficial to low-income and minority Americans. Typically, low-income Americans start paying Social Security taxes at an earlier age than other workers. Yet this is not reflected in their benefits. It would be with an IRA, however, since the longer compounding period would mean a greater accumulation of retirement savings. The Ferrara plan would also guarantee benefits to low-income retirees under the SSI program, financed by general revenue. The elderly poor, in other words, would not have to depend on the financial viability of an unsound payroll-based system for their retirement income.

The average life expectancy of a black male aged 25 today is such that he can expect to receive benefits for only 5 months, while a white male of the same age can expect 6 years of full benefits—about 15 times as much.[12] With an IRA-based system, however, the black male could choose to retire early with a full annuity or leave his accumulated retirement savings to his survivors.

The Ferrara plan is a version of a standard technique of privatization—the buy-out. Faced with a federal program in which projected benefit obligations are in excess of projected revenue, the traditional budget-cutter attempts either to cut benefits, which alienates beneficiaries, or to increase program revenues, which alienates contributors by reducing their expected returns. The privatizer, however, seeks to wind down the federal program, buying out existing obligations by giving individuals an incentive to seek a private alternative, and then spreading the buy-out costs as widely and thinly as possible.

A Political Strategy

It is clear from the history of Social Security policymaking that merely putting forward a rational and carefully conceived reform plan—even one as cogent as that proposed by Peter Ferrara—is not likely to achieve much. As noted earlier, expert analysis of Social Security's failings has been rejected in the past in favor of political pragmatism. There is little reason to suppose that logical argument will win the day in the foreseeable future. Indeed the Ferrara plan was given short shrift by the 1982 National Commission on Social Security. A fundamental reform proposal, by itself, is of little interest to practical politicians.

If a privatization strategy is to be successful in moving Social Security into the private sector, it must be based on a full appreciation of the political dynamics of the system. Strategists must never forget that there is a firm coalition behind the system. But unlike the coalitions behind other programs, the constituency behind Social Security does not include service providers (since it is a cash-benefit program), and that does make the task a little easier. The beneficiaries, however, constitute one of the most powerful political forces in America. And that political force is driven both by fear and by a sense of righteousness: the fear of older Americans that they might be left destitute in their retirement, and the widespread but erroneous belief that Social Security benefits constitute a fair return on an individual's "savings" in the form of payroll deductions.

The fear and righteous indignation felt by older workers and retirees makes the Social Security system virtually impregnable to any frontal attack. Populist politicians can pounce on any structure reform proposal, and they can inflame elderly Americans by appealing to their financial worries and their sense of justice. Moreover, younger Americans have a natural and proper concern for the elderly. Even if they are skeptical about the long-term health of the Social Security system (and opinion polls show clearly that they are), very few young people show a strong desire to end the intergenerational transfers of wealth implicit in Social Security if that poses a threat to the elderly.

If Social Security is to be restructured and its enormous drain on federal spending reduced, the strategy must include plans to defuse the emotion within the Social Security coalition and to break the bond that holds it together. Without that step, any attempt to identify a private alternative to Social Security and to construct a coalition around it will be unsuccessful.

Weakening the Social Security Coalition

The steps most likely to weaken the Social Security coalition would be a "customized buy-out" and an effective challenge to the notion many Americans have of the quality of Social Security benefits compared with the available alternatives. The goal of these steps would be to calm the fears of part of the coalition and to encourage its other members to seek their retirement needs through private options—in other words, to divert their demand out of Social Security.

1. Guarantee the benefits of the elderly

A privatization approach could calm the fears of the retired, and those about to be retired, by providing them with an absolute guarantee that specified benefits will be fully paid. But instead of simply making a declaration to that effect (retired Americans have been burned sufficiently often to distrust such solemn declarations), privatizers should seek constitutional protection for benefits, thereby outflanking the Social Security lobby.

Such a step can be justified on both moral and political grounds. Although the Social Security system may have been poorly designed and based on flimsy actuarial principles, it nevertheless contains an implicit contract with the elderly. Millions of Americans have based their retirement financial planning on the assumption that they will receive certain benefits. Those already retired and workers nearing retirement cannot be expected to adjust their financial affairs drastically because the other party to the contract has been irresponsible. Moreover, a guarantee would also make sound political sense. Accepting existing benefit obligations as a write-off takes the issue out of the political picture. Instead of instilling panic among the elderly, privatizers could discuss a reform proposal in more rational terms.

At the moment, Social Security benefits have no constitutional protection. The Supreme Court held, in 1960, that under current law, Social Security benefits are not constitutionally protected-as are returns from U.S. government bonds, for instance. The court held that Congress can cut off Social Security benefits at any time, just as it can terminate any other spending program.[13]

As Peter Ferrara has pointed out, however, the Court's decision was based on its interpretation of the statutory intent of Congress in setting up the program. And so that decision can be reversed by a statutory change.[14] Such a change should be sought from Congress, to the effect that current retirees and workers within, say, ten years of retirement would be entitled to a U.S. government bond guaranteeing continued payment of the benefits available under the law at that time, constantly adjusted for inflation, throughout the person's retirement years. This benefit structure would reflect the preretirement income of most Americans. For very low income Americans, the bond would be a safety-net income funded from general revenues. This would provide Social Security bondholders with the same constitutional protection as holders of any U.S. Treasury bond.

It is easy to see why this would be an attractive proposal to organizations of retirees, and it is difficult to see how legislators could find it in their political interests to oppose it. But once achieved, the step would clear the way for other proposals designed to buy out other key elements of the coalition.

2. Individual Statements of Account

Under the existing regulations of the SSA, it is practically impossible for the "contributors" to the Social Security program to discover what rate of return they can expect on their taxes so that they can compare that figure with the tax rate a private pension or insurance plan would allow. A worker who writes to the appropriate official at the SSA, and is honored several weeks later with a reply, will simply be told the total amount he or she has paid into the system. No estimate will be provided regarding the likely rate of return. SSA officials do not provide that kind of data.

Because such information is unavailable, the typical worker has no means of comparing Social Security with an IRA, private disability insurance, or any other form of private retirement protection. Not surprisingly, myths abound. Those elderly people who were well into their working life when Social Security began no doubt believe that they are simply obtaining a fair return on their contributions, whereas they are receiving many times a reasonable return on the money they "invested." Many young workers express doubt that the Social Security system will still be intact when they retire, but probably few of them realize that even if it does endure, they can look forward to a near-zero or even a negative return. And certainly, too few young black Americans realize that their comparatively low life expectancy means that they may collect just a few months of benefits in return for their taxes—meaning that they will, in effect, be supporting white Americans throughout their working years.

The administration could dispel these myths by instructing the SSA to establish an individual account for each participant in the program. Each worker would then be provided with an annual statement showing what contributions he or she had paid into the system and the rate of return implied by the likely stream of future benefits.

The SSA claims that it cannot provide such information to workers because it has neither the staff nor the computer capacity. That is perhaps just as well. SSA staff would have every incentive to paint a rosy picture of the future benefits and every reason to avoid using actuarial classes that could be embarrassing to the SSA's thesis that Social Security provides reasonable and equitable retirement benefits. It would be to contract the task out to life insurance companies and other financial institutions well versed in risk analysis and economic forecasting.

In this way, each working American would receive a summary of his or her Social Security taxes for that year, plus a running total for previous years, broken down into contributions to retirement and premiums for health, disability and Medicare insurance. The insurance coverage would be specified and the rate of return on the pension contributions estimated according to stated economic assumptions and the worker's actuarial class. With this information in hand, the contributor would have the data he needed to compare the Social Security coverage with the dozens of alternative IRA and insurance plans advertised every day in his local newspapers.

As with the constitutional guarantee for current beneficiaries, it is difficult to see how effective opposition could be mounted to such a move by an administration. "Surely Americans have a right to know what they can expect from their tax contributions?" privatizers could ask of their critics. "Surely they have a right to compare these with what is available elsewhere?" Such an innovation would be "consumerist" in the best sense. And it would do much to encourage some key elements of the Social Security constituency to look hard at more attractive private alternatives.

3. Detaching Middle-Aged Workers

Middle-aged and older workers who have made substantial tax payments into Social Security have little incentive to support reform proposals that might threaten their retirement income. So they have good reason to denounce any politician who talks of reducing the return they expect from their contributions. They also have an incentive to endorse proposals that would pay for their benefits by increased payroll taxes falling most heavily on succeeding generations of workers. This strong vested financial interest in the existing system makes them a powerful element of the Social Security coalition.

One way to reduce this group of workers' enthusiasm for Social Security would be to offer them a bond that would entitle each worker to a retirement annuity in proportion to the tax contributions he or she has made into the system. These workers would then be able to place all or part of what would have been their future payroll taxes into more attractive Super IRAs in the way proposed by Ferrara.[15]

Workers who opted for the bond would then have a greater incentive to support moves to expand private-sector, IRA-based alternatives to Social Security, and correspondingly less incentive to defend the current system.

4. Detaching Younger Workers

Younger workers pose a dilemma for the privatizer. On the one hand, they are the easiest group to detach from the Social Security coalition with the lure of a private-sector alternative. They have less money already invested in the system, and an individual account would indicate to them that a private plan would provide many times the return they could expect from Social Security. Opinion surveys also indicate that they are pessimistic about the chances that the system will ever provide them with any benefits.

On the other hand, if young workers were to leave Social Security in droves—as they might well do, given the opportunity—it would place enormous financial pressures on the system because tax revenues would be reduced for many years before substantial reductions were achieved in outlays, assuming credits were taken against payroll taxes. Ferrara's phase-out plan would keep this need for general revenue support to below $40 billion, but it could still lead to significant taxpayer opposition.

There are two ways of resolving this problem. The first, as noted earlier, would be to allow workers opting out of Social Security to credit their contributions against their income tax, not their payroll tax. This would have the advantage of spreading the cost across the entire population, assuming additional taxes or borrowing were needed to address the income tax shortfall. But it would have the political disadvantage of seeming to many to be the equivalent of general revenue finance, perhaps opening the floodgates to such support on a large scale and practically guaranteeing that Social Security would expand further.

A second way of resolving this dilemma would be to learn from the experience of Britain and Chile, each of which has a partly privatized system. Britain, as John Goodman has explained, has allowed workers to opt out of Social Security since 1960.[16] In 1978, however, Britain embarked on a comprehensive opting-out plan, with the support of both major parties.

Britain now has a two-tiered Social Security system. The first tier is mandatory and provides a basic minimum pension. The second tier provides a pension based on earnings and is voluntary. Private companies, not individuals, can opt out of this tier if they establish a plan for their workers at least as good as the state system. Since 1978, reports Goodman:

> more than 45% of all British workers have contracted out of the second tier pension scheme. Moreover, by allowing the option of contracting out, the British government has effectively cut its second tier pension liability in half. Overall, I estimate the government has reduced its entire Social Security liability by more than 30% by adopting the contracting-out system.[17]

In Britain, contracting out takes place at the company level. In Chile, individuals can opt out of Social Security if they put at least 10% of their income into the equivalent of an IRA. Workers who opt out receive bonds to cover their past contributions. Within seven months after the opting-out provision was put into place, almost half of all Chilean workers had exercised that option.

The most interesting aspect of these two examples, from the perspective of an American strategy, is not so much that a remarkable proportion of workers decided to opt out, but that under both plans they still have to continue paying part of the Social Security tax even though they receive no benefit from it. In Britain, for instance, the payroll tax was reduced from 18.5% to 11.5% for workers choosing to opt out of the second tier. For the average-income worker after 20 years of employment, Goodman calculates, this means that state pension benefits fall by almost half for just a 38% reduction in payroll tax.[18] In Chile the payroll tax is reduced from 27% to 17%.

This means that workers in Britain and Chile are prepared to pay what amounts to an opting-out tax to escape from part or all of the Social Security system. In Chile, political and economic instability might well have induced workers to opt out of a state-run program at almost any price. But in Britain, with its welfare-state tradition, the willingness of workers to give up benefits while paying taxes, in order to exercise the private-sector option, is particularly interesting—and the opting out program commands solid union support.

The dilemma of how to allow younger American workers to opt out of Social Security, and thereby reduce liabilities, without undermining the finances of the system (because of massive payroll-tax losses) may well be solved by using an opting-out tax approach. If the British experience is any guide, it might be possible to induce large numbers of young workers to opt out of Social Security in favor of a Super IRA, and to forgo Social Security benefits, while requiring them to continue paying one-half or one-third of the taxes they would pay to remain fully within the system.

Naturally it would be much fairer to allow workers to take a full credit for any contribution they placed into an IRA rather than in Social Security, and thereby relieve liability pressure on the system. But the system is in such imbalance that a substantial intergenerational transfer is unavoidable if Social Security is to honor existing commitments. And the opting-out terms do not have to be accepted. Rational workers will accept them only if they feel that they will do better in the private sector than they could in the public sector. The opting out tax does not mean workers would not gain by exercising their right to choose, only that they would not gain as much. But the tax would mean that the need for direct or indirect general-revenue support would be reduced.

Fostering the Private-Sector Coalition

As explained in Chapter 2, weakening the public spending coalition is only half of the two-pronged privatization strategy. The various buy-out proposals recommended above would help to weaken the Social Security coalition and thereby improve the political atmosphere for moving much of the program into the private sector. But the second prong of a privatization strategy requires the creation of a countervailing private-sector coalition to lobby for a steady expansion of the private sector option. It was noted that various methods can be used to promote such a coalition. For instance, permitting private-sector organizations to compete with the government and then providing targeted tax incentives to encourage use of the private option changes the cost differential between the public and private sectors and diverts demand out of the public sector.

The IRA is a good example of the privatization tax incentive that can act as the stimulus to the formation and expansion of a private-sector coalition. It is a true mirror image of the spending catalysts that cause federal budgets to grow. Tax-deductible pension accounts give a concentrated tax benefit to individuals who choose to utilize this method to provide themselves with retirement protection. If this causes people to reduce their demand for government services by an equivalent amount, then the government, and hence the taxpayer, will come out ahead in the long run, since the government will lose less in tax revenues than it will gain in reduced spending commitments (the ratio will depend on the individual's tax bracket). But even if, for the sake of argument, we assume that an IRA deduction will require all other taxpayers to pay more to cover a net shortfall, the political balance will still favor the holders of IRAs. They have a strong financial interest in maintaining the deduction (worth up to $1,000 each year to those in the top tax bracket), while the "cost" is spread widely and thinly among all taxpayers. Consequently, IRA holders have every incentive to lobby hard for the deduction, while the average American without an IRA has little to gain by pressing for the deduction to be denied to others.

This political imbalance helps to entrench such privatization catalysts, causes a coalition to grow around them, and encourages that coalition to lobby for the expansion of the incentive. What appears to be a minor tax change, in other words, sets political forces in motion that create the momentum for radical change. This process is likely to make the IRA a powerful vehicle for privatizing Social Security.

The political dynamics are already evident. IRAs for the general public have been far more popular than Treasury officials assumed when legislation allowing them to be used by all taxpayers was enacted in 1981. The corresponding tax revenue losses to the Treasury have also far exceeded the official estimates made at the time. Nevertheless, the popularity of IRAs has insulated the deduction from any political threat. Some politicians and officials complain that IRAs are draining away potential tax revenues, causing an increase in the deficit. IRAs, they claim, merely rearrange savings accounts and do not add to them, but no leading politician would risk advocating that the IRA deduction be eliminated. IRAs have even crept into the list of "untouchable" deductions that most flat-tax proponents retain in their proposals to cut drastically the "loopholes" and tax shelters in the tax codes.

The beginning of a campaign to expand the deduction is already under way. Amid the intense effort to find ways of increasing taxes in the spring of 1984, Congress was giving serious consideration to proposals to expand the IRA deduction. With the backing of the administration, the Senate actually passed a measure that would phase in the same annual deduction for nonworking spouses that is available to working taxpayers. The extension was removed in a House-Senate conference compromise only so that agreement could be reached on spending reductions.

Groups of beneficiaries and service providers are also beginning to express interest in expanding the IRA into a more comprehensive pension vehicle. These groups include the National Taxpayers Union, a 1.2-million-strong grass-roots lobbying organization; the National Alliance of Senior Citizens; and the half-million-member National Federation of Independent Business, the country's leading small-business organization. Moreover, the banking, investment, and insurance industries are taking an increasingly close look at the long-run potential of the multibillion-dollar IRA business.

If this potential coalition is to be galvanized into an effective constituency for private Social Security, privatization strategists must remember the lessons of the expansion of Social Security itself: Incrementalism works, but grand designs generally do not. As noted earlier, the foundations of the Social Security system were enacted in 1935, but disability insurance, health insurance, and other elements of the program were added gradually over several decades. Although some scholars and interest groups envisioned a comprehensive system during the debates in the early 1930s, Congress and the nation were unwilling to adopt such a sweeping change at once. Indeed, if congressional supporters of the 1935 legislation had possessed the ability to see how Social Security would expand, no doubt many of them would not have voted for it.

The same is true of a private Social Security system. A complete plan such as Ferrara's may be elegant and carefully structured, but it frightens people. It is too comprehensive and sweeping for most Americans to take in one dose—and hence it is difficult for their representatives to endorse it. Even the service industries that could gain much from handling the finances of a comprehensive private system hesitate to back it publicly for fear of seeming to threaten the Social Security system. So at the moment, proposals for a completely private Social Security system are of interest primarily to scholars, not politicians.

A private-sector system will develop slowly, perhaps over many years, as strategists take each opportunity made available to press forward expansionist proposals they add more constituencies to the coalition. The more small tax and regulatory changes they can obtain to increase the attractiveness of private-sector alternatives, the sooner the political dynamics will begin to favor the privatization coalition, enabling major reform to take place. At each point in this incrementalist strategy, privatizers must take care not to threaten the beneficiaries of the existing system, and thus invite political backlash. Each new proposal put forward must be an acceptable alternative—or even an addition—to some element of the current system, and individual Americans must be given time to accept it.

A possible strategy of incrementalism is already taking shape. The first step—allowing an equal IRA deduction for homemakers—has already begun to emerge as a women's issue. Nonworking spouses are an obvious group of near-beneficiaries who have much to gain from that small extension of the IRA deduction. In the political atmosphere of the 1980s it is unlikely that such an equality demand can be resisted for long.

Another small proposal that would advance the strategy would be the conversion of the existing tax deduction into a tax credit set at the same level as the after-tax value of the deduction for the highest income earner—$1,000 for a taxpayer in the 50% bracket. A $1,000 income tax credit for an IRA would make the retirement accounts far more attractive to lower-income taxpayers and would thus draw a new and key group into the IRA constituency. If this proposal was accompanied by the release of further studies indicating the inequities regarding the poor and minorities inherent in Social Security's benefit structure, the political support for an IRA credit could be widened and intensified.

Just as Social Security took major steps forward with the additions of disability and Medicare components, expanding IRAs by permitting new deductions or credits for additional services could garner strong support for a private system. A "Medicare IRA" appears to be a distinct possibility on the horizon. Concern is already growing that the federal Medicare system will run into serious financial difficulties within a decade. And there is almost a panic among many of the nation's older workers that they will be unable to avail themselves of the remarkable advances in medical technology because Medicare and their personal savings will be insufficient to pay the bills. Consequently, an addition to the tax-free IRA ceiling for the purchase of retirement medical insurance to supplement Medicare is likely to prove increasingly popular as fears about the adequacy of Medicare become more intense.[19]

By advancing such modifications of the basic IRA, it should be possible to move slowly toward a Super IRA that would provide the same range of insurance and benefits that are now available under Social Security. At each point in the debate a group of near beneficiaries and service providers would have a financial interest in seeing the IRA expanded. These individuals would have the incentive to join forces with the existing IRA beneficiaries and service providers to campaign for an expansion of IRA coverage. And just as the political dynamics tend to favor coalitions supporting spending programs, because benefits are concentrated while costs are thinly spread, so there would be a tendency for the IRA coalition to prevail in the political contest. Moreover, with an expansionist private-sector coalition in place and growing stronger with each small legislative victory, one could expect a strong campaign to be mounted by the coalition to persuade workers to choose the private option, and heavy lobbying pressure to make crossing over as attractive as possible.

The difference between this privatization strategy and conventional "cures" for Social Security spending is critical. Conventional budget-cutting attempts to persuade the patients to take unpleasant medicine—in other words, cut back on their benefits. This means that responsible politicians must take something away from the public. By so doing they must face an uneven contest with the public spending coalition that gains most from the program. Privatization, on the other hand, allows politicians to offer the citizens an attractive private alternative and the right to choose it if they wish. Nobody is forced to do anything, but the citizen is rewarded for demanding the private option. In addition, by concentrating benefits on those who choose the private option and on the firms that deliver the private service, politicians also know they are encouraging the formation and growth of a coalition that will alter the political balance, enabling radical reform of Social Security to take place and reducing the cost of the system.

7

THE FUTURE OF PRIVATIZATION

The privatization proposals discussed in the preceding chapters indicate ways in which a general political strategy can be adapted to very different types of federal programs. In each instance the goal of the technique under discussion is to change the dynamics now favoring increased public spending. Privatization does this by breaking up or otherwise weakening each coalition benefiting from the federal program by planting the seeds of a new coalition that would benefit from nongovernment delivery of the service.

Altering the dynamics in this way would improve the prospects for traditional supply-side budget cutting—that is, reducing the size of government by winning congressional agreement for program cutbacks. A successful privatization campaign means budget cutters would face far less powerful opposition to their proposals, because part of the demand for government provision would have been diverted into the private sector.

It is impossible to gauge the likely budget impact of a full-scale privatization strategy, because privatization is a political approach aimed at altering the underlying dynamics powering long-term budget growth. It is not a set of specific spending targets designed to achieve immediate, but probably short-lived, program cuts. Privatization seeks instead to replace the federal ratchet with a private-sector ratchet, so that the balance of power shifts decisively away from those who want government to grow and toward those who want it to shrink. Some of the proposals put forward, such as selling public housing, would yield immediate improvements in the budget picture, but most proposals would provide long-term solutions to deep-seated structural budget problems.

The general objectives and techniques of the privatization strategy were discussed in Chapter 2. They provide the battle plan and arsenal for the budget cutter. But if federal spending is to be controlled and then cut, strategists must appreciate that two additional steps must also be taken. These involve changing the spending incentives that exist at the state and local levels and also giving the privatization effort a clear focus at the federal level, so that it can acquire the institutional momentum necessary for continued success.

The State and Local Dimension

Altering spending incentives at the state and local level is necessary for effective privatization for two reasons. In the first place, it must be remembered that reducing the size of the federal sector is important because that reduction serves to reduce the burden placed by government on the private sector. If federal spending reductions are merely replaced by state and local spending increases, that is still a step forward. As explained in Chapters 1 and 2, shifting programs down the federal ladder does tend to put a brake on government growth, since the closer the taxing and spending functions of government are to the people, the greater is taxpayer scrutiny and resistance to inefficient spending. But state and local spending is still government spending, and so the burden on the private sector continues. Consequently, any mechanisms the federal government can put in place to encourage privatization at the state and local level would help to reduce the total level of government spending.

The second reason for examining ways to stimulate privatization at lower levels of government is that politicians and other elements of local public spending coalitions often lobby for increased federal outlays simply because federal incentives encourage them to do so. Voters will often support local public expenditures because "free" federal money makes the total bill to the citizen lower than that charged by a less costly private provider who must charge full expenses to the community. Mayor Edward Koch of New York, for instance, has had every reason to urge the construction of Westway, the highway running down the West Side of Manhattan, despite a price tag that could top $10 billion if the road is completed. The reason: 90% of the cost of the project is to be picked up by the federal highway trust fund. The same federal program encourages cities to defer routine maintenance, and thus keep local taxes down, so that they can qualify for federal money for new construction once a road or bridge deteriorates significantly. Similarly, mass transit assistance encourages cities to choose expensive public transport over cheaper private alternatives, just as federal development grants make it politically attractive for city leaders and developers to campaign for more public projects.

As long as the design of federal assistance programs subsidizes public spending at the state and local level, while requiring private alternatives to charge their full cost, government programs will tend to be the more attractive alternative. Steps should be taken, therefore, to change the incentive structure to encourage the use of private services at the state and local level, thereby relieving pressure for federal spending as well as that by lower tiers of government.

Several methods could be used to do this. One would be to put pressure on states to modify rules and regulations that discourage privatization by threatening to withdraw funds if states do not comply. The federal government has been successful at enforcing the 55 mph speed limit by using this tactic, and more recently Congress used the same approach to force states to raise the drinking age. But threatening the states in this way is not always successful: Congress balked at the Reagan administration's attempt to end rent control by adding a no-control requirement for the receipt of housing money. When politically practical, however, the approach is very effective. For instance, it might well be the appropriate method of forcing states to simplify occupational licensing laws, to open up new sources of human services, and to reduce restrictions on private bus systems and other private approaches to mass transit.

The federal government could also use the antitrust laws to prevent municipalities from erecting barriers to private competitors to government-funded services. Since 1978 the Supreme Court has begun to use the Sherman Act to stop local governments from thwarting such privatization. Unfortunately the Reagan administration has failed to appreciate the importance of antitrust suits in furthering privatization: Persuaded by the principle of local "freedom," it supported a bill to prevent damage awards against municipalities engaging in efforts to monopolize services and restrict competition.[1]

A combination of the carrot and stick can also be used, rather than the stick alone. Many federal assistance programs to state and local governments, such as waste water treatment capital grants and human-service grants, discourage private alternatives by laying down specific designs or excessively tight qualifications. Streamlining these federal rules, like pressing for a simplification of state and local rules, would make private alternatives more attractive at the community level. Grants could also be made contingent upon local experiments in privatization, to foster the creation of privatization coalitions. Or cities could be allowed to keep a portion of the federal savings that accrue from the switch to a private provider. Under budget pressure, state and local governments have already begun extensive contracting out of services such as garbage collection, fire protection, and park maintenance.[2] Federal incentives could accelerate this and other forms of privatization.

Another way in which the federal government could encourage private sector action at lower levels of government would be through changes in the tax code, and in tax aspects of federal grant programs, to end the code's discrimination against private services. The payment of state and local taxes to finance government services, for instance, can be deducted from taxable income for federal tax purposes. But if a homeowner pays a fee to a private garbage collector or other service provider, that fee is not deductible. So although the private service could cost much less than the publicly provided service, the after-tax "price" of the government service to the homeowner could well be lower. This discrimination against privatization would be removed by allowing fees for private services to be deducted from federal taxable income. At the very least, such fees should be made deductible to the extent that they qualify the taxpayer for a rebate from local taxes.

The federal government could also institute tax incentives for approaches that reduce the demand for state and local projects financed through federal programs. The enterprise zone proposal, for instance, is designed to stimulate economic development in depressed inner city neighborhoods by reducing regulation and taxes on economic activity.[3] Such incentives bring growth through private capital formation and enterprise, and so they constitute a private alternative to local economic development projects financed with federal money, such as Urban Development Action Grants or the Community Development Block Grant.

Providing tax incentives restricted to certain areas, incidentally, not only encourages citizens to choose private development methods over government-financed projects but also sows the seeds of a privatization coalition of businesses and their employees. Beneficiaries within the zones press for deeper incentives, and near-beneficiaries lobby to be included in the program. At the end of 1984 the enterprise zone proposal was still awaiting congressional action. But the strong support it has acquired in the Congress and the fact that about half the states have jumped the gun and created their own zones with state tax relief indicate that concentrated tax benefits can generate powerful lobbies for shifting even antipoverty programs into the private sector.

The federal government could consider various other ways of using the tax code in this way to relieve the demand for state and local services and, indirectly, for its own programs. The charitable deduction, of course, already does this by encouraging the support of local community initiatives.

Yet the federal government could give a further stimulus to such initiatives by offering "matching relief" for state tax incentives aimed at aiding private development or human-services projects, just as general revenue sharing provides federal funds to states according to their "tax effort"—that is, how heavily they tax their residents. Some states, such as Missouri, allow corporations to take a 50% tax credit against state income taxes for contributions to approved projects that constitute a "neighborhood assistance program." But such state tax relief is taxable at the federal level. If federal tax relief were to be given to state tax incentives intended to foster privatization, it would not only be a justifiable mirror image of the tax effort concept of federal assistance, but by helping to reduce the demand for development and human services at the local level the policy would also relieve state pressure on federal funds.

Institutionalizing Privatization

Important though it is to find ways of encouraging privatization at the state and local level, the top priority must be to build the strategy into the institutions of the federal government so that its techniques become a basic ingredient of budget policymaking.

The best way to accomplish this, while protecting the integrity of privatization, would probably be for administration proponents of the strategy to practice what they preach—that is, to "privatize privatization." As noted throughout this book, government officials and the research organizations that work closely with government have a predisposition to favor government solutions over private solutions to problems. So if the White House were to invite federal departments to suggest candidates for privatization from among their programs, the list would probably be short. Even officials strongly committed to private alternatives often find great difficulty in obtaining research and civil service backing they need from within their own departments.

An independent task force or commission on privatization, given permanent status and reporting directly to the president, might therefore be the most effective way of institutionalizing the privatization strategy. During the first Reagan administration, the President's Private Sector Task Force on Cost Control (the Grace Commission) brought together teams of business executives who applied hard-nosed analysis to government programs, free of the constraints that apply to any internal civil service search for savings. Consequently, the commission was able to find billions of dollars in budget reductions that could be made to improve the efficiency of federal programs. Unfortunately, the Grace Commission was not asked to design a political strategy to carry out its recommendations, so its report had a cool reception on Capitol Hill—and even in some areas of the Reagan administration.

A privatization commission should reflect the political lessons learned from the Grace Commission. In particular, such a commission should attempt not merely to identify potential candidates for privatization but also to indicate possible means to achieve privatization. In each situation it should identify the private-sector coalition that would benefit from privatization. The commission should then recommend ways to weaken the existing public-sector coalition (such as buy-outs or licensing changes to promote competition) and ways to strengthen the privatization coalition (such as targeted tax incentives).

To accomplish this task, a privatization commission would have to be carefully structured. Reflecting the need for research on alternative private service providers, the commission should include representatives of research institutions not closely associated with the federally supported research industry. And bearing in mind the importance of practical political initiatives for successful privatization, it would also need to recruit members from among those with first-hand experience of the process of government, while avoiding those who still have political ambitions.

To aid further the work of the commission, the president should make sure the group has the necessary cooperation of key parts of the government. Close liaison between commission researchers and the research arms of federal agencies would be an important step, so that White House-backed recommendations could be made to departmental officials regarding research to further the privatization strategy. Steps should also be taken to enable the commission to identify regulatory barriers to privatization. One way to do this would be for it to work with rule-making staff in each agency. But perhaps a better approach would be to revive the Vice President's Task Force on Regulatory Reform, to aid the commission by giving it more influence within the government and top-level support for its activities. Finally, the work of the commission would be significantly enhanced if teams were made available from the Treasury and the Office of Management and Budget, to assist in identifying possible tax incentives, candidates for privatization, and ways of incorporating privatization techniques into the overall budget strategy.

Creating a permanent and independent commission to make privatization recommendations would not, of course, insulate the strategy from pressures emanating from the public-spending coalitions. In particular, the benefits of a working relationship with segments of the government would have to be weighed against the possibility of cooption by officials who have become advocates for federal programs. But it should not be forgotten that a commission examining privatization possibilities would also tend to become a focus for influence by groups likely to gain from privatization-and those groups would be quick to help the commission find ways to strengthen privatization coalitions.

An independent, private task force making budget cutting recommendations would be a major departure from the traditional budget-making process. But the failure of governments in America to cut spending stems in large part from a reluctance to be creative. When the Reagan team came to Washington in 1981, it scored some impressive budget victories based on David Stockman's blueprint, thanks to political boldness and the momentum for budget reductions generated during the 1980 election. But when the public-spending coalitions regrouped and began to fight back, the Reagan administration did not significantly change its tactics. It still came charging up the hill to Congress, hoping to achieve budget reductions by political arm-wrestling. After 1981, however, the opponents of cuts had become well entrenched and quite able to withstand the siege.

When Mrs. Thatcher assumed office in Britain in 1979 a different process developed. There was no immediate success in reducing spending like that enjoyed by Reagan, but the government began a systematic experiment with various methods of budget control. When a technique was successful, the government pursued it further. If it ceased to be effective, another approach was tried. It was from this trial and error approach that privatization emerged in Britain. The government stumbled into privatization and it worked.

If federal spending is to be brought under control in America, enabling the deficit to be cut without crippling increases in taxation, new political strategies must be attempted to change the dynamics of budget growth. Privatization holds out the prospect of finally breaking the federal spending ratchet and replacing it with a private-sector ratchet, so that the pressure to spend is reduced by diverting demand away from government programs. If the administration is willing to experiment with the device, and thereby turn the flank of the public spending coalitions, it could achieve a historic reversal of the growth of government in America.

Notes

Chapter 1

1. Richard P. Nathan and Fred C. Doolittle, *Effects of the Reagan Domestic Program on States and Localities* (Princeton, N.J.: Princeton Urban and Regional Center, 1984).

2. Milton Friedman and Rose Friedman, *Tyranny of the Status Quo* (San Diego, Calif.: Harcourt Brace Jovanovich, 1984), pp. 30–33.

3. Ibid., p. 34.

4. "David Stockman: No More Big Budget Cuts," *Fortune*, February 6, 1984, p. 54.

5. Ibid.

6. For a critical analysis of the theory that deficits increase interest rates, see Thomas Humbert, "Understanding the Federal Deficit: The Unproven Impact," Heritage Foundation *Backgrounder* No. 330 (Washington, D.C.: Heritage Foundation, 1984).

7. "Friedman Fears Economic Growth, Slide," *Washington Times*, June 2, 1983.

8. James Q. Wilson, *Political Organizations* (New York: Basic Books, 1973), p. 330.

9. Ibid., p. 332.

10. S. Robert Lichter and Stanley Rothman, "What Interests the Public and What Interests the Public Interests," *Public Opinion*, April/May 1983.

11. Stanley Rothman and S. Robert Lichter, "Are Journalists a New Class?" *Business Forum*, Spring 1983.

12. Ibid.

13. James Q. Wilson, "The Rise of the Bureaucratic State," *The Public Interest*, No. 41 (Fall 1975), p. 89.

14. Ibid., p. 88.

15. Quoted in Martha Derthick, *Policymaking for Social Security* (Washington, D.C.: Brookings Institution, 1979), p. 24.

16. Ibid., p. 110.

17. Lester Salamon and Alan Abramson, *The Federal Budget and the Nonprofit Sector* (Washington, D.C.: Urban Institute Press, 1982), p. 44.

18. Carl Milofsky, "Professionalism in Community Organizations," *Community Action*, Vol. 1, No. 3, 1982.

19. Derthick, *Policymaking*, p. 26.

20. Quoted in Derthick, *Policymaking*, p. 26.

21. Wilson, *Political Organizations*, p. 333.

22. Lester Salamon and Alan Abramson, *The Federal Government and the Nonprofit Sector: Implications of the Reagan Budget Proposals* (Washington, D.C.: Urban Institute, 1981); Charles Clotfelter and Lester Salamon, *The Federal Government and the Nonprofit Sector: The Implications of the 1981 Tax Act on Individual Charitable Giving* (Washington, D.C.: Urban Institute, 1981).

23. J. Peter Grace, *President's Private Sector Survey on Cost Control: A Report to the President* (Washington, D.C.: Privately printed, 1984).

Chapter 2

1. Madsen Pirie, *Dismantling the State: The Theory and Practice of Privatization* (Dallas: National Center for Policy Analysis, forthcoming).

2. Ibid.

3. See also Sandy McLachlan, *The National Freight Buy Out* (London: Macmillan, 1983).

4. Pirie, *Privatization*.

5. E. S. Savas, *Privatizing the Public Sector* (Chatham, N.J.: Chatham House, 1982), p. 56.

6. Ibid., Chapters 3 and 4.

7. Ibid., p. 55.

8. Peter Berger and Richard Neuhaus, *To Empower People: The Role of Mediating Structures in Public Policy* (Washington, D.C.: American Enterprise Institute, 1977).

9. "Public Services in Private Hands," *Venture*, July 1984, pp. 34–44.

10. See, for instance, *Passing the Bucks: The Contracting Out of Public Services* (Washington, D.C.: American Federation of State, County and Municipal Employees, 1984).

11. *Enhancing Governmental Productivity through Competition: A Progress Report on OMB Circular No. A-76* (Washington, D.C.: Office of Management and Budget, 1984), p. 7. OMB maintains that the threat of contracting out a specific government activity has encouraged significant efficiency improvement within the agency itself.

12. Ibid., p. 10.

Chapter 3

1. John C. Weicher, "Halfway to a Housing Allowance?" in his *Maintaining the Safety Net* (Washington, D.C.: American Enterprise Institute, 1984), p. 105.

2. John C. Weicher, *Housing: Federal Policies and Programs* (Washington, D.C.: American Enterprise Institute, 1980), p. 56.

3. For a more thorough description and analysis of the British program, and a discussion of strategies for America, see Stuart M. Butler, "Public Housing: From Tenants to Homeowners," Heritage Foundation *Backgrounder* No. 359 (Washington, D.C.: Heritage Foundation, June 1984). Legislation passed in 1983 raised the discount to 60% for tenants who have lived in public housing for 30 years.

4. "In Housing Policy, It Seems the Tories Had a Winner," *New York Times,* June 22, 1983.

5. *Ladies' Home Journal,* July 1984.

6. Susan A. Marshall, *Public Housing and Mediating Structures: The Case for Tenant Control* (unpublished reference paper, Washington, D.C.: American Enterprise Institute, 1984).

7. Congressional Budget Office, *Federal Subsidies for Rail Passenger Service: An Assessment of Amtrak* (Washington, D.C.: U.S. Government Printing Office, 1982), p. 25.

8. Ibid., p. 26.

9. Ibid., p. xx.

10. Jeffrey Shedd, "Amtrak: Congress's Toy Trains," *Reason*, May 1981.

11. CBO, *Federal Subsidies*, pp. 60, 61.

12. Ibid., pp. 13, 31.

13. John Semmens, "End of the Line for Amtrak," Heritage Foundation *Backgrounder* No. 226 (Washington, D.C.: Heritage Foundation, November 1982).

14. CBO, *Federal Subsidies*, p. 21.

15. Quoted in CBO, ibid., p. 32.

16. Shedd, "Amtrak," p. 28.

17. Ibid., p. 24.

18. Adding in long-term avoidable costs would swell losses by about 22% per year, according to the 1982 CBO analysis. Long-term avoidable costs are those that could be eliminated over several years if a route were closed down, such as the cost of maintaining locomotives and rolling stock.

19. U.S. Department of the Interior, Bureau of Land Management, *Public Land Statistics* (Washington, D.C.: U.S. Government Printing Office, 1979).

20. Robert H. Nelson, *Seeking Alternatives to Federal Land Ownership*, unpublished paper, National Conference of the American Society for Public Administration, April 8–11, 1984, p. 41.

21. Ibid., pp. 43–44.

22. Richard L. Stroup and John Baden, *Natural Resources: Bureaucratic Myths and Environmental Management* (San Francisco: Pacific Institute, 1983).

23. John Baden and Richard L. Stroup, "Saving the Wilderness," *Reason*, July 1981, p. 33.

24. Bruce Ramsey, "Forest Socialism," *Reason*, December 1983.

25. Quoted in Ramsey, ibid., p. 34.

26. Ibid.

27. Quoted in Gordon T. Lee, "What If the Government Held a Land Sale and Hardly Anybody Showed Up?" *National Journal*, September 25, 1982, p. 1624.

28. Nelson, *Seeking Alternatives*, p. 76.

29. Quoted in Ramsey, "Forest Socialism," p. 34.

30. Ibid., p. 35.

31. Luke Popovich, "Free Enterprise Zones in the Sticks?" *Journal of Forestry*, February 1984, p. 92.

32. Nelson, *Seeking Alternatives*, p. 85.

33. Ibid., pp. 86–87.

34. Robert J. Smith, "Conservation Capitalism," *Libertarian Review*, October 1979, p. 21; Baden and Stroup, "Saving the Wilderness," pp. 33–34.

35. John Baden, "Privatizing Wilderness Lands," in Phillip N. Truluck, ed., *Private Rights and Public Lands* (Washington, D.C.: Heritage Foundation, 1983), p. 68.

36. Steve Hanke, "Land Policy," in Richard Holwill, ed., *Agenda '83* (Washington, D.C.: Heritage Foundation, 1983), p. 190.

Chapter 4

1. Figures from John C. Weicher, ed., *Maintaining the Safety Net* (Washington, D.C.: American Enterprise Institute, 1984), p. 4, based on various editions of the *Budget of the United States Government*. It should be noted that figures for human-services spending often include many programs, such as Social Security, which are not restricted to low-income people. Weicher's calculations do not include such programs, but they do include Aid to Families with Dependent Children, Supplemental Security Income, low-income home energy assistance, the earned income tax credit, housing assistance, food assistance, Medicaid, training and education, and social services.

2. Ibid.

3. Ibid., p. 17.

4. Richard P. Nathan and Fred C. Doolittle, *Effects of the Reagan Domestic Program on States and Localities* (Princeton, N.J.: Princeton Urban and Regional Center, 1984).

5. Ibid., p. 3.

6. John Herbers, "States Finance Aid Programs Reduced by U.S., Study Finds," *New York Times*, June 10, 1984.

7. James Bovard, "Feeding Everybody: How Federal Programs Grew and Grew," *Policy Review*, No. 26, Fall 1983.

8. Eileen Gardner, "The Education Crisis: Washington Shares the Blame," Heritage Foundation *Backgrounder* No. 351 (Washington, D.C.: Heritage Foundation, 1983).

9. "Despite the Soup Lines, the Statistics on Hunger Remain Elusive," *Washington Post*, December 24, 1984.

10. Lester M. Salamon, *Nonprofit Organizations and the Rise of Third-Party Government,* paper presented to the Independent Sector Research Forum, May 1983, pp. 13–15.

11. Ibid., pp. 28–33.

12. Robert L. Woodson, "Helping the Poor Help Themselves," *Policy Review*, No. 21, Summer 1982, p. 77.

13. Ibid., pp. 85–86.

14. Peter L. Berger and Richard J. Neuhaus, *To Empower People* (Washington, D.C.: American Enterprise Institute, 1977), pp. 36, 37.

15. Virginia Tuman, "Day Care Laws Limit Private-Home Centers That Parents Like Best," *Wall Street Journal*, October 26, 1982.

16. Woodson, "Helping the Poor," p. 74; Woodson, "When Will We Free Our Children?" *Detroit News,* February 12, 1984.

17. Diane Brockett, "D.C. Foster Care Hit in New Study," *Washington Star,* February 24, 1981.

18. Jack A. Meyer, "The Unfinished Agenda in Health Policy," in Weicher, *Safety Net*, p. 74.

19. Medicare, of course, is a part of the Social Security program and not an element of the human-services budget targeted to low-income Americans. Nevertheless, the economic incentives implicit in the programs, and hence the implications for public policy, are substantially the same. The annual Medicare bill is roughly three times the federal outlay on Medicaid.

20. William A. Schambra, "From Self-Interest to Social Obligation: Local Communities v. the National Community," in Jack A. Meyer, ed.,

Meeting Human Needs (Washington, D.C.: American Enterprise Institute, 1982), p. 38.

21.   Ibid., p. 42.

22.   Ibid., p. 48.

23.   Peter L. Berger, "Toward an Alternative Vision of the Welfare State," *Catholicism in Crisis*, November 1983, p. 20.

24.   Ibid.

25.   Ibid.

26.   Ibid., p. 21.

27.   Ibid., p. 22.

28.   Marsha Levine and Denis P. Doyle, "Private Meets Public: An Examination of Contemporary Education," in Meyer, *Meeting Human Needs,* pp. 286, 287.

29.   Joan Davis Ratteray, *Alternative Education Options for Minorities and the Poor*, unpublished paper to the National Center for Neighborhood Enterprise, Washington, D.C.

30.   Ibid., p. 2.

31.   Woodson, "Helping the Poor," p. 78. For a full account of the House of Umoja, see Woodson, *A Summons to Life* (Cambridge, Mass.: Ballinger, 1981).

32.   Woodson, "Helping the Poor," pp. 80, 81.

33.   John Herbers, "Cities Turn to Private Groups to Administer Local Services," *New York Times,* May 23, 1983.

·34.   For a discussion of this point, see Stuart M. Butler, "Grassroots Partnerships: New Alliances for Inner-City Renewal," *Economic Development Commentary*, Vol. 6, No. 4, Winter 1982.

35.   For a discussion of donation patterns, see Stuart M. Butler, *Philanthropy in America* (Washington, D.C.: Heritage Foundation, 1980).

36.   See Meyer, "Unfinished Agenda," pp. 74, 75.

37.   See E. S. Savas, *Privatizing the Public Sector* (Chatham, N.J.: Chatham House, 1982), pp. 67–69, 143–45.

38.   Berger, "Alternative Vision," p. 22.

39.   Robert W. Poole, Jr., *Cutting Back City Hall* (New York: Universe Books, 1980), p. 129.

40.   John McClaughry, "Who Says Vouchers Wouldn't Work?" *Reason,* January 1984.

41.   Harry Hatry, *A Review of Private Approaches for Delivery of Public Services* (Washington, D.C.: Urban Institute, 1983), p. 43.

Chapter 5

1. James Q. Wilson, "The Rise of the Bureaucratic State," *The Public Interest*, No. 41, Fall 1975, p. 84.

2. Ibid.

3. General Accounting Office, *The Post Office Can Substantially Reduce Its Cleaning Costs* (Washington, D.C.: U.S. Government Printing Office, 1982), AFMD-83-23.

4. Peter M. Kendall, "World Mail Centers Will Zip All of Your Mail to Its Destination," *National OTC Stock Journal*, December 23, 1983.

5. James Bovard, "The Last Dinosaur," *Policy Review* (forthcoming).

6. James Bovard, "Getting the Mail to Sail," *Wall Street Journal*, August 6, 1984.

7. See, for instance, Robert Poole, "Is This Any Way to Run a Postal Service? No," *Wall Street Journal*, October 11, 1982.

8. Bovard, "The Last Dinosaur."

9. Bovard, "Getting the Mail to Sail."

10. General Accounting Office, *Replacing Post Offices with Alternative Services* (Washington, D.C.: U.S. Government Printing Office, 1982), GGD-82-89, p. 7.

11. John Crutcher, "The Privatization of the Postal Service," *Washington Times*, June 2, 1983.

12. Milton R. Copulos, "The Perils of a NASA Space Monopoly," Heritage Foundation *Issue Bulletin* No. 109 (Washington, D.C.: Heritage Foundation, 1984), p. 3.

13. "Medicine Sales Forecast at $1 Billion," *Aviation Week and Space Technology*, June 25, 1984, p. 52.

14. Quoted in ibid., p. 79.

15. Ibid., p. 116.

16. Christopher Madison, "Federal Subsidy Programs under Attack by Unlikely Marriage of Left and Right," *National Journal*, December 31, 1983.

17. Robert W. Poole, Jr., "Air Traffic Control: The Private Sector Option," Heritage Foundation *Backgrounder* No. 216 (Washington, D.C.: Heritage Foundation, 1982), p. 2.

18. Ibid.; see also "Towards Safer Skies," in Robert W. Poole, Jr., ed., *Instead of Regulation* (Lexington, Mass.: Heath, 1982).

19. Breton R. Schrender, "Some Small Airports Hiring Firms to Provide Air-Traffic Controllers," *Wall Street Journal*, March 24, 1982. See also John Doherty, "Towering Entrepreneurs," *Reason*, May 1983.

20. Robert W. Poole, Jr., "How to Ground Plane Delays," *Reason*, September 1984.

21. Larry Phillips, "Time to Change Our Stalling Air Traffic Control System," *Wall Street Journal,* July 5, 1984.

22. Poole, "Traffic Control," p. 14.

23. Phillips, "Time to Change."

24. Poole, "How to Ground Plane Delays."

25. Dina Rasor, ed., *More Bucks Less Bang* (Washington, D.C.: Fund for a Constitutional Government, 1983), p. 7.

26. Quoted in Seymour Melman, *Pentagon Capitalism* (New York: McGraw-Hill, 1970), pp. 12–13.

27. Wilson, "Bureaucratic State," p. 87.

28. Office of Management and Budget, *Enhancing Government Productivity through Competition: A Progress Report on OMB Circular A-76* (Washington, D.C.: U.S. Government Printing Office, 1984).

29. Dina Rasor, "Fighting with Failures," *Reason,* April 1982.

30. Quoted in Melman, *Pentagon Capitalism,* p. 231.

31. Rasor, "Fighting with Failures," p. 28.

32. "Procurement Success Story," *Wall Street Journal,* February 6, 1984.

33. Rasor, *More Bucks,* p. 9.

34. See, for instance, Jennifer Hull, "Cracks are Forming in Business' Support of Defense Spending," *Wall Street Journal,* August 17, 1984.

Chapter 6

1. For a discussion of the politics surrounding the creation of the Social Security system, see Carolyn L. Weaver, "The Economics and Politics of the Emergence of Social Security," *Cato Journal,* Vol. 3, No. 2, Fall 1983.

2. Martha Derthick, *Policymaking for Social Security* (Washington, D.C.: Brookings Institution, 1979), p. 288. Cited hereinafter in text.

3. The most recent "rescue" plan, passed by Congress in 1982, added two more groups of workers into the system—newly hired federal workers and the employees of tax-exempt organizations. Again, the short-term effect will be an inflow of revenue to help cover existing liabilities, but the long-run effect will be a further increase in the liabilities of the system. This means that some future Congress will have to find additional revenue to cover the benefit commitment.

4. A. Haeworth Robertson, "The Underlying Problems of Social Security," in Peter Germanis and John Palffy, eds., *Rebuilding Social Security* (Washington, D.C.: Heritage Foundation, 1982). pp. 5, 9; Robertson, *The Coming Revolution in Social Security* (McLean, Va.: Security Press, 1981), chapters 6, 7.

5. Peter J. Ferrara, *Social Security: The Inherent Contradiction* (San Francisco: Cato Institute, 1980).

6. Peter J. Ferrara, "Rebuilding Social Security: Part 1: The Crisis Continues," Heritage Foundation *Backgrounder* No. 345 (Washington, D.C.: Heritage Foundation, 1984), pp. 3–5.

7. Peter J. Ferrara, *Social Security Reform* (Washington, D.C.: Heritage Foundation, 1982).

8. Ibid., p. 4.

9. That is, Old Age, Survivors, Disability and Hospital Insurance.

10. Ferrara, *Social Security Reform*, p. 76.

11. Ferrara, Rebuilding Social Security, Part 1, p. 7. Ferrara notes that this is based on returns after all business taxes are paid. A fairer comparison would be based on the real before-tax returns available from private investments, which is closer to 12%.

12. *The Effect of the Social Security System on Black Americans* (Dallas: National Center for Policy Analysis, 1983).

13. *Flemming* v. *Nestor*, 363 U.S. 610.

14. Ferrara, Rebuilding Social Security, Part 2, p. 2.

15. For a general discussion of bad proposals see Ferrara, *Inherent Contradiction*, pp. 340–50.

16. See John C. Goodman, *Social Security in the United Kingdom: Contracting Out of the System* (Washington, D.C.: American Enterprise Institute, 1981); Goodman, "Lessons from Abroad," in Germanis and Palffy, *Rebuilding Social Security;* Goodman, "Private Alternatives to Social Security: The Experience of Other Countries," *Cato Journal*, Vol. 3, No. 2, Fall 1983.

17. Goodman, "Private Alternatives," p. 568.

18. Ibid., p. 567.

19. The National Center for Policy Analysis has put forward a proposal for a "Health Bank IRA", as part of a general reform plan for Medicare. The proposal calls for an annual tax credit of $500. See Peter Ferrara, John C. Goodman, Gerald Musgrave, and Richard Rahn, *Solving the Problem of Medicare* (Dallas: National Center for Policy Analysis, 1984).

Chapter 7

1. Clint Bolic, "Use Antitrust Law Against Local Government Offenders," *Wall Street Journal*, August 16, 1984.

2. For a summary of local services that have been privatized, see Harry Hatry, *A Review of Private Approaches for Delivery of Public Services* (Washington, D.C.: Urban Institute, 1983); E. S. Savas, *Privatizing the Public Sector* (Chatham, N.J.: Chatham House, 1982); Robert W. Poole, Jr., *Cutting Back City Hall* (New York: Universe Books, 1980).

3. For background on the enterprise zone concept, see Stuart M. Butler, *Enterprise Zones: Greenlining the Inner Cities* (New York: Universe Books, 1981).

Index

Kemp-Roth tax-cut proposal, 5
Kenilworth-Parkside housing project, 71–72
Kennedy, John F., 12, 146

"Liberal view of federalism," 10, 11
Licensing requirements, as obstacle to privatization, 24, 102
Line-item veto, 32
Load shedding, 52–53, 56
Local governments. *See* State and local governments
"Low-budget Great Society," 94–96

Mass transit assistance, 13, 167–68
Media
  how used to support increased spending, 24, 29
  in building support for privatization, 47
Medicaid, 56, 93, 99, 103–4
Medicare, 14, 18, 56, 103–4, 117, 146–47
Meyer, Jack, 103, 104, 115
"Micropolitics," as key to privatization, 44
Myers, Robert, 22, 25

Nader, Ralph, 17, 114, 132
National Aeronautics and Space Agency (NASA), 11, 121–22, 128–31
  See also Space program
National Audubon Society, 88, 89
National defense
  as a collective good, 49, 121, 136
  contracting out, 54, 55, 136–39
  factors inhibiting competitive bidding, 139
  the Pentagon as a bureaucracy, 138
  procurement process
    reform of, 141–42
    separating research and development from, 139–40
  reasons for high cost, 137–38
  spending on, 6
National Education Association (NEA), 102, 108, 118
National Space Transportation System (NSTS), 128, 129, 131 *See also* Space Program
New Deal, the, 12, 92
New Federalism, 50, 95

Office of Management and Budget (OMB), 5–6, 171

PATCO strike, 122, 133, 134, 136
Pirie, Madsen, 34, 35, 44
Pollution controls, 14
Poole, Robert, 133–35
Postal Service, *See* U.S. Postal Service
President's Private Sector Survey on Cost Control. *See* Grace Commission
Private goods, 49
Private sector coalition. *See also* Coalitions
  fostering the formation of, 60–62, 108–12
  importance to privatization, 4, 46–48, 86, 94, 132
  need for better organization, 61
Private sector ratchet, as key to privatization, 43–48, 172
Private sector spending, versus government spending, 13, 105–6
Privatization
  approaches to, 52–57
  budget impact of, 166
  commission on, need for, 170–72
  future of, 166–72
  in Great Birtain, 33–43, 172
  incremental approach, 61–62 163, 164
  informal privatization, 87–88
  institutionalizing, 170–72
  principles for implementation, 44–48, 57–62
  through sale of publicly owned corporations, 37–40
  as solution to neighborhood problems, 109–12
  strategy for, 113–19
  versus supply-side approach, 44
  See also Great Britain, privatization in
Property rights, *de facto,* 86, 88
Public housing, 66–75
  expenditures on, 66, 67
  impact on neighborhoods, 68
  importance of ownership, 68, 69
  original purpose of, 66, 67
  privatization of
    in Britain, 40, 46, 68, 70
    opposition to, 70, 72–73
    prospects for future, 74–75
    tenant management, 71–74
    See also vouchers
  right-to-buy laws, 74, 75
  sales to tenants, 40, 46, 69